Guns of Ava

THE KEN DULA STORY

Bullets devastated his body.
She devastated his heart.

BRENDA ROSE WOMBLE

This book is creative nonfiction. Much of the background and incidents of the story are based on fact as clearly as it could be recalled. However, names and character descriptions are purely fictitious. Any character resemblance to persons, living or dead has no relations to real people. Chapter 11 is the actual account.

DEDICATION

This book is dedicated to my deceased mother, Rosa (Rose) Lindsey, who was always my greatest fan. She taught me that if you are grateful for the small things, big things will come your way.

Thanks to God for his inexplicable grace for writing!

ACKNOWLEDGEMENTS

First and foremost, to my best friend, Ken, for allowing me to write his amazing story. I gained invaluable knowledge about the life of a soldier. Night after night, endless hours of burning the midnight oil, telephone calls, and insurmountable meetings over dinner or a quick lunch was worth it, because your story was worth telling. After listening to you, my appreciation for combat soldiers and all men and women in uniform who've served and are still serving in this great nation has increased even more. You are my hero!

To my wonderful son, Dedrick, who always believed in me and never complained even through the tough places of our lives. When the ballroom lights went out, you reminded me that there was yet another dance to come. I love you! And thank you, dear Kimmie, for my first book on creative writing. So much needed!

To my friend and partner in business, Stephie Ann, who worked so diligently to see my work printed. You will never know how much I appreciate you!

To Mary Matthews, who assisted with my first writer's conference of the Mediterranean seas to Rome, Italy. How could anybody have writer's block while sailing? Thank you for believing in my dream. And to my colleagues and students at North Carolina Central University, what a joy to hear you ask, "How is your writing coming along?" Thanks for caring. And Dr. Ogede, what a blessing to have your feedback after intensive reading.

To my niece, Vicky, for lending an ear to my ideas no matter how often they changed. And, to my niece, Regina, who always advertise my accomplishments. To my entire family (particularly my surviving siblings, Ann and Lib), who support me in all of my endeavors.

To my friend, Sylvia, who stood by me in Santa Fe, New Mexico, throughout my pitch sessions and brought meals to me every day. I will never forget you. To my deceased friend, Beth, for the loan of her beach house as a get-away to write. What a book signing party you would've given me! I will never forget my deceased friend, Bernard, who fussed but always fixed my computer when it crashed (very often) so I could keep on writing. Wish you both were here.

To my deceased friend, Robin Parker, who kept me encouraged by repeatedly saying, "Hurry and get this done, so I can buy my dress for the red carpet." I know you are looking down from heaven and still rooting for me.

To Janis and Annette, who listened to my endless readings and read the painful rough drafts of my first chapters. I'm so thankful. Alease, you never cease to amaze me with your strength and tenacity! Thank you for that shoulder when I needed it. Bert, what prayer will do! You were that bridge over troubled water. My feet never got wet. Thank you my friend, Vanessa, for reading every word of my final draft! I will buy you new glasses if you need them.

To my editor, Ellexia. Thanks for your patience and expert advice. To Mariji for making adjustments no matter how often I changed my mind. And, Janice, thanks for the prayers and laughter along the way. I needed that.

And, to my interior designer, Heather, I pray for a pair of golden angel wings when you get to heaven. Thank you for working so hard.

Finally, to you, the reader who felt an irresistible tugging to purchase my book. That was me. Without you, I'm done. Thank you.

CHAPTER 1

The day I left for basic training, I cried with her. I never thought eight weeks later, I'd cry because of her. It was the truth I came home for on that cold February day. I guess I should've known better than to let her get to me like that, but I'd never been in love before. Up until then, I thought you could control how far love takes you. But it wasn't long before I learned this simple truth—that you can get caught off guard and love impinges on you. Before you know it, you're there, helplessly lost in its power.

I left Fort Bragg that day around noon for my home town of Lenoir, North Carolina. After spending an hour with my family, without a shower or change of clothes, I headed to Ava's place. My father had no idea what was on my mind when he offered me his car.

"I'll drive to the barber shop and you can take the car to see your gal," he said. "I'll pick it up later. You think she can bring you home?"

"Yes, I'm sure she won't mind."

I hopped in the passenger seat of my father's pride and joy 1965 Rambler. My father never let anyone drive his car, but for some reason, I was privileged to get it that day.

He sat in the driver's seat, adjusted his mirror and backed out.

The two-lane highway was heavily traveled, making it difficult for him to pass or drive any faster. I kept glancing at my watch and wished I'd driven, but he insisted on taking the wheel.

About a mile from home, he started talking about the Korean War and how hard it was for him to leave my mother when he was my age. He was never a talker, but that day was different. He wanted to spill his guts on me.

I thought maybe he felt comfortable talking to me, now that I was walking in his shoes—a foot soldier, serving in the United States army. But, no disrespect to him, I wasn't listening. I couldn't keep my mind off the conversation I'd have with Ava and the dreaded outcome.

I sneaked another peak at my watch. Jeez! He was driving fifty-five miles per hour. My father was the most law-biding citizen I'd ever known.

His voice lowered and his expression changed to that of deep thought as he recalled the cold war. He repeated himself a couple times, saying it was the deadliest war in the history of the world. His memory was serving him well, even though so many years had passed. A deep sadness came into his voice as he spoke of his comrades and the men he saw die. "They're fellows I'll never forget," he confided to me.

I nodded and stared ahead at the thick traffic. This trip is taking too long!

A steady build up of dark clouds loomed above the mountain top. In the distance, thunder rumbled. The sky looked ready to release a huge downpour at any moment. My luck wasn't looking good. I knew if a storm got us, the traffic would move even slower, and so would my father.

"You never heard my war stories before now, right?" he asked. I shook my head and gave a perfunctory smile.

"Well, all the same if you haven't," he said. "You'll know what I'm talking about sooner or later." He paused and glanced over at me. "How long you home?"

"Just a few days," I said. "When I return, I'll go into A . . ."

"AIT. I know," he grunted. "Then you're going to Vietnam. Sounds 'bout right."

He cleared his throat and spoke in the tone of voice he used when I was a freshman in high school and needed to be reminded of my curfew.

"When you get to Nam, just remember to never let your guard down," he said. "And try to keep your mind off your gal." He gave a light chuckle as if he knew how badly I wanted to see her.

Heavy drops of rain splashed on the windshield. Seconds later, they stopped as quickly as they came. My father rattled on. "I got through it and you will, too," he said. "Times will be hard, but be a good soldier and do your job. Keep your head on straight. Your brothers and sisters look up to you."

Fearing he would think I wasn't paying attention to him, I resisted the urge to look at my watch a second time.

Finally, my father looked satisfied that he'd said all he wanted to say. He stared ahead in silence.

We came to a traffic light and stopped. My eyes held his for a couple of seconds when he said, "Be strong and keep your head on straight." His eyes were gentle, speaking to me in a way words could not. It was then I knew why he insisted on driving me. It was to get me alone to have a sincere father to son conversation. All of his talk was to let me know he was concerned, if not worried, about my welfare. It still wasn't clear as to why I was able to get his sacred automobile.

I peered out of the window into the heavens. The clouds had scurried away, leaving behind the blue sky. I figured God knew how badly

I wanted to get to my destination. He must've held back the storm just for me.

The traffic light flicked green, and we sped along. Before long, he pulled into the parking lot of where he cut hair. He handed me the keys.

"Have fun with your gal." He let out a big chuckle.

I grabbed the keys and rushed to get to the driver's side. Finally, travel would be a lot faster, now. I had the wheel.

"Leave the keys in the glove compartment," he yelled."I shouldn't be here, long."

I threw up my hand and drove off. About five minutes later, I neared the street where Ava lived. My heart started to pound and a migraine— like the ones I used to get when I was young, the kinds that left me in bed for days— pinched the corner of my forehead.

I turned the corner. Two buildings down stood the place I was so accustomed to visiting. I turned the motor off, stuck the keys in the compartment, and jumped out. Taking two steps at a time, I reached the front porch of the two-bedroom apartment.

I gave a couple of light taps to the door. While I waited, my mind drifted to the first time I saw her in town. She looked like someone you'd see on the cover of Vogue magazine. Her jet black hair bounced at the slightest toss of her head. As she walked past me, her petite body made slow strides, causing a nice twist in her hips. She moved as though she knew I was watching. And it was true. I couldn't keep my eyes or hands off of her, later on after our first date. Now, nearly two years later, she still had that effect on me.

I knocked harder, and then through the thin curtains that hung slightly apart at the front door, I saw movement.

The door flung open. And there in front of me stood the first woman who'd ever stolen my heart. Her bare shoulders were exposed in a T-strap blouse showing her dark, silky skin like an African goddess. A few hair rollers were stacked on top of her head. Widened with surprise, her eyes met mine.

"Ken! What on earth are you doing home?"

She stood frozen for a second or two. Then she wrapped her arms around me. It felt good to hold her—to feel her small frame next to me. I pulled her closer and buried my face into her hair. I loved the familiar sweet fragrance of honeysuckle that lingered after one of her fresh shampoos. Her warm breath fanned my cheeks, making me weak. At that moment, I thought about the real reason I had rushed to see her. My body stiffened. I tried to push back the ill thoughts, but they were lodged there, right in the forefront of my mind.

She stepped back and opened the door wide.

"Come on in," she said.

I walked inside. The coat rack in the hallway held her scarf she'd carry every time we'd go to the lake. The short denim coat she wore the last night we were together hung next to it.

She rushed in front of me with the same exciting twist of her hips as the first day I saw her. Making her even sexier, she had on a short skirt that clung to her hips. The corners of my mouth quivered from the thrill of watching her.

"Wait right here," she said. "I forgot to turn off my curlers." She headed down the hall and called over her shoulder. "There're cold drinks in the fridge."

Amid all of the uncertainty floated a pleasant smell I recognized. It was coming from the kitchen. I always got carried away by the scent of her thick hamburgers. She made the best in the world and took them every time we picnicked at the lake.

"You should've told me you were coming home," she called from her bedroom.

"It wouldn't have been a surprise, would it?" I yelled back.

"Luckily, I have your favorite on the stove," she said.

I heard a door shut down the hall. I scouted the room and my eyes fell on the mantel over the fireplace. The baseball I had autographed for her when my high school team won third place in competition rested against a stack of books. Beside it was a photo of the two of us on a hiking trip. Perhaps things weren't as bad as I had imagined. She would've removed all memories of me if that were the case.

I moved across the room to the sofa. My mind went to the night I knelt nervously in front of her. It took guts to ask her to go steady with me. We both had just turned seventeen that year. I was a couple of months younger. Lots of guys at school asked her out, but she refused. Some of them, who'd dated more women than you could count, told me she liked older men—preferably three or four years. I later found out they said that only to discourage me from seeing her and it almost worked. I felt I was out of the running and nearly gave up the chase.

Howard, my best friend and confidant, who was always successful in finding a steady girl, eased my mind. "It's not the age that's important," he said. "It's the way you have to talk to them. They like to hear things that make them feel good inside. And what woman doesn't like an athlete? That's what my dad told me."

I wasn't as husky as some of my team players. But I didn't look bad at 5'10" and a drop below 170 pounds with a six-pack body frame from working out and playing sports. I was a conservative dresser and wore good smelling cologne. Many girls had their eyes on me. However, Ava had all of my attention. I'm not sure what it was about me that impressed her. But whatever it was, it certainly paid off.

A noise from the back pulled my attention. I looked toward her bedroom and wondered what was taking her so long. As I started down the hallway, she met me halfway. Her rollers were out, and her hair nicely tucked in a bun. I was alone with Ava with my thoughts and the stillness of the room.

She stood in front of me. The moment seemed awkward. I noticed she was wearing the necklace I gave her for her birthday. It was expensive for a fellow who didn't make a lot of money, but she was worth it.

She started toward the kitchen. I walked behind her and took a quick glance down the hall. I stopped and pulled her to me.

"Can we just talk?" I asked. "I haven't seen you for a long time, you know."

She smiled. Her hazel eyes danced as she looked back at me. She took my hand, sauntered back into the living room over to the sofa and sat down with her buttocks hugging the edge of the seat. "Look at you . . . you look great," she said. Her eyes traveled down my torso and back to my face.

I knew she loved men in uniform. She told me one time it was seeing me in my baseball suit and cap that made her want to date me. I was certain my army fatigues were more impressive than my baseball attire.

I stood over her and studied the curve of her lips and caught the sparkle in her eyes. I wanted to pull her back in my arms, kiss her over and over and not let go. But first, I had to know the truth—good or bad. And I knew I would get it, because lying had never been one of her strengths.

"Well, are you going to just stand there?" she asked.

I sat down beside her with my arm over the back of the sofa—perfect for her to snuggle, I thought. Without any coercing on my part, she always cuddled up to me. However, this time, she didn't move a muscle. I'd never scrutinized her before. I never needed to do anything as such. But now I was observing every tiny detail—the shifting of her eyes, her restlessness, and her quick statements that suggested she wanted to keep the subject off her and on me.

She shifted positions to face me.

"So, when are you leaving for Vietnam?" she asked. "I heard on the news that more soldiers were leaving next month."

Enough! I'd had enough with the small talk. The conversation was sounding more like an interview for a job. I didn't want to talk about the news, the weather report, or how I was fairing in the military. I was ready for the truth.

"Look," I said, as I leaned into her face. "I'm not sure what's going on, but I got some information that I don't like." Her eyes held a puzzling look as I got straight to the point.

"Have you been seeing somebody?" I asked. She looked as if I'd slapped her with the back of a skillet.

"Who told you that?" she asked, shaking her head from side to side.

"Please, don't lie to me," I demanded.

I held my firmness, determined not to let her sweet, loving and unassuming voice get to me. I wanted to believe that it wasn't so, but as hard as I tried, I couldn't get rid of the encroaching thoughts that suggested she was lying.

"I want to hear it from you," I said. "I want the absolute truth. Have you been seeing someone since I've been gone?"

She didn't reply. She didn't have to. Silence said it much better than words. Blood rushed to my head, making me dizzy. Through stiff lips and tightly clenched fist, I stood and walked the length of the floor, stopping at the fireplace.

I stared at the space on the carpet where we used to make out. Intrusive thoughts raced in my head. I'd imagined this stranger—I'd heard about—lying on a blanket beside her. He'd stolen precious moments we'd shared. I could see him holding her, kissing her tender lips and caressing her soft flesh where my hands belonged. He had discovered the secrets of our intimacy and heard her panting short breaths in his ear. He'd watched her fall asleep in his arms as he held the body that was only accustomed to my touch.

"Who is he?" I asked, with my back to her.

She still didn't answer. I'd never hit a woman in my life. I didn't believe in it. However, I wanted to punch something—anything, just not her. I pounded my fist hard against the wall. I wasn't the vociferous or cussing kind of guy, either. I came from a family with a Pentecostal mother who had put the fear of God in me and my siblings, so deeply that we thought just saying the word "hell" would send us there. And although our father was not religious like our mother, I never once heard him utter one word of profanity.

I took in a deep breath and turned to Ava.

"You promised me you'd wait for me," I said.

I ran my fingers hard across my forehead as if it were possible to press away the thoughts of her and another man. Our world had been invaded by this stranger. But a stranger would need permission to occupy someone's dwelling, wouldn't he? Unless, of course, he entered by force. She didn't wear the appearance of a distraught female who'd been violated, but one who'd been caught being unfaithful. I wasn't a saint or a priest of any kind, though it would have been helpful for me at the time. Perhaps I would've stopped to consider what Jesus would do. Instead, I reached for the necklace. She grabbed my hand and held on to it, tightly.

"Don't take it," she pleaded. Her voice was nearly inaudible. "Please let me explain."

I saw the desperate look on her face as she pleaded. Even in her weakest moment, with her mascara smeared in the corner of her eyes and a few strains of hair clinging to her wet cheeks, she looked strikingly beautiful. I wanted her in my arms. Oh, God! What was I going to do without her?

One quick jerk and the necklace fell to the floor.

"Please . . . oh, please," she cried. "It's not what you think."

Her hair that was tucked neatly into a twist on top of her head dropped to her shoulders as she slid onto the sofa. A couple of fresh curls fell over her face, covering her tearful eyes. Her voice escalated into a pitiful cry.

"You don't understand," she said, as a gush of tears washed away her fresh makeup. "Let me explain."

I held the necklace to her face.

"Didn't this mean anything to you?" I asked. "I spent everything I had on this for you . . . for you! Because I loved you. All of me loved you."

I fought back a bucket of tears. I can't break down, I thought. Not now. I can't let her see how badly she'd hurt me. I can't let her have the upper hand in this. My head was spinning. Why was the love that once blazed between us turning into a low, quiet flame? We'd vowed never to be unfaithful. She'd promised to be right there when I returned. Now, in one second, I was driven crazy, and I hadn't even heard her out. I didn't want to listen to her story. I'd just opened her secret closet and had seen her ugly dress of deception.

I threw the necklace across the room and stormed out. The screen door slammed hard behind me as I rushed onto the porch. Did I love her too much? Did I give her too much of my love and affection? A line from a poem I'd learned years ago popped in my head. "Be careful not to water the plant too much. Too much care can kill it." Had I showered her with so much tenderness that I destroyed us? Of course, not! It couldn't explain why she would secretly throw herself into the arms of another man.

I left her front porch and noticed my father had already gotten the car. I started walking toward town. As I glanced back at her place, I saw her standing at the window with the curtains slightly parted and her face pressed against the glass. I wanted to go back and let her talk, but the egotistical male inside instructed me not to do it. I wondered if my rush to judgment would come back to haunt me.

About five minutes down the highway, I decided to thumb a ride. Several cars whizzed by. With my luck, I thought, it would be well after midnight before I'd get home.

My rapid steps kept up with the racing of my heart. After about a mile, a red pickup truck loaded with heavy metal equipment stopped.

"Need a ride?" a friendly trucker asked.

I nodded and hopped inside the passenger's seat. The dark-skinned black man looked to be in his forties. He wore a cowboy hat with a plastic straw hanging in the corner of his mouth.

"Where you heading, soldier?' he asked.

"Dula Town," I said.

"Oh, yeah," he said. "I'm going in that direction."

The radio blasted some R&B music. He tapped his steering wheel and whistled along with the song. Out of the corner of my eye, I saw him looking at me.

"Got drafted?"

I nodded.

"My son did, too," he said. "But, if all goes well, he'll be out next month for good.

"Lucky man," I said.

I was astonished by how calm my voice was—how I had managed to hold in the depth of my anger about the draft, along with my disappointment about Ava. I had hopes of returning, after I served my time in the war, as her knight on a white horse in shining armor. I had plans of sweeping my darling right up and riding off into the sunset. Sadly, instead of the magical white horse, I was riding home in a rusty pickup with a stranger as my companion. And the fragmented pieces of my broken heart were left scattered on her living room floor.

I stared out of the window and saw nothing—nothing but the face of the woman I loved buried in my mind. A face filled with guilt and shame.

"Are you all right?" the man asked, as he eased off the gas pedal.

"Right now, I don't know," I answered.

"Let me guess," he said. "Female problems."

I nodded.

"Yep," he said. "I knew I called it right. I swear I don't think I'll ever figure a woman out, and that's the God in heaven truth. In my house, PMS wears the pants and that ain't no lie!" He laughed.

I tried to smile at his humor, but my cheeks felt like they were holding a bucket of rocks. I thought I'd never have to worry about a broken heart. Several of my friends had girls to walk out on them, and I'd given them advice that seemed fairly simply. "Don't react," I'd urged. "Sleep on it, and the next day you'll see things in a better light." That's what I told all of them. And now I couldn't heed to my own counseling.

The man sped up. "It's best to get along with them, 'cause you can't never win or please 'em," he said.

I didn't answer. He switched the radio station to a sports channel and the conversation turned to baseball, a topic that always got my interest.

Before long, I was in my parents' driveway. I opened the door and our dog, Tubby, ran to greet me. He seldom barked, but this time he kept yelping like he knew something was wrong.

"How much do I owe you?" I asked the driver, as I slid out of the seat.

"Not a thing," he said. "You just get out of this damn war without getting killed, and that will be all right with me."

I shook his hand and watched him drive away. Tubby stopped barking and tilted his head up at me. I knelt down and stroked his back.

"I know you will never leave me, my old faithful friend," I said.

I dropped down beside Tubby and thought back to the image of Ava at the window. The pitiful look had pushed away the sweet, laughable face that held so much joy. I pulled Tubby to me and rubbed his head. I looked over at the horizon. The sun was sinking behind the low hanging clouds. Daylight was fading and what Ava and I had was disappearing with it. Why didn't I see this coming? But I couldn't have. There was never a hint.

"It can't end like this, Tubby." I muttered. "Not now, not ever. I have to go back."

CHAPTER 2

For about an hour, I sat on the steps with my dog. I recalled the day I got my letter that involuntarily enlisted me in the United States army. I couldn't help but blame the White House for what had happened to me and Ava. If I hadn't been selected for military duty, I would've been near her each day, giving her all the love she'd ever wanted. There would've been no chance for this stranger—this snake in the grass—to slither in.

The draft was ludicrous to me. I was confounded at the decisions made by governing officials in the White House. How could they sleep at night after forcing us young people into a war on foreign soil for a cause that none of us understood?

I reflected on the day I got my letter. I was in a very good mood that day. I had made plans to take Ava out to dinner, and afterwards, we were going to watch a movie at the downtown drive-in theater. But we never got there. As soon as I walked in the house from my part-time job, my mother handed me an envelope.

"It looks important," she said.

I looked at the return address that read, "United States Army." I knew immediately what was inside. I think my mother knew, too, because she started humming. She always hummed when something was on her mind.

A sudden surge of heat swept through me. No one—not even Howard, who I shared my soul—knew how much I feared the draft. I'd stopped watching the evening news. Every single day, there were more gruesome reports about the war in South Vietnam. My father kept track of the current conditions and would tell me what was happening. I was sure his military background fed into his need to keep me informed.

My mother's humming never ceased as I tore open the envelope. I sat frozen as I read the words that would soon turn my life into a horror movie.

"What does it say?" she asked.

I was speechless. A few seconds later, I handed the letter to her. My mother pulled her glasses from her apron and read it.

"You're drafted," I heard her whisper.

She dropped her head and closed her eyes. She always got quiet like that when she was talking to God. Growing up, I used to think each night she had a board meeting with him and the angels. Her prayer sounded much like gibberish, making no sense to me as she spoke in what she called an "unknown tongue." But whether I understood it or not, I knew she got results from God.

When she finally spoke, her voice was calm and reassuring. "I knew this would happen," she said, as she stuffed the letter back in the envelope and reached for my hand.

"But, you'll be fine, son," she said. "I had a dream and the good Lord showed me you'd go to war. You'll be wounded, but not killed."

Killed? That word shot through me like an arrow. Sweat popped out profusely on my forehead. I had no plans of going anywhere to get myself killed. My thoughts spiraled like a cyclone into outer space. I got up and ran outside.

I thought about a couple of my friends I'd graduated with from high school who'd received letters. Amazingly, Howard didn't get one, because he was the only child. I thought since I hadn't heard from Uncle Sam, somehow I'd escaped, too.

I got to my car, and the hood caught me as my knees buckled underneath. I kept telling myself not to panic. I had to be strong for Ava.

After a moment or two, I got in my old jalopy with one headlight missing and headed to her apartment. On the way, I kept slowing down as I tried to wrap my head around the fact I was going to be leaving Ava.

When I arrived, I steadied myself and took a few seconds before I tapped on her door. Immediately, it flung open. Ava looked amazing. She was dressed in her blue jeans and matching jacket. Her face was full of excitement, and she was ready to go. But, when she saw I wasn't smiling, her cheeks dropped.

"What's wrong?" she asked.

I brushed past her into the living room and fished for the right words to say. Things were going perfectly. At the time, I'd just finished Barber College and started barbering. I was bent on trying out for professional baseball. I was certain I'd get selected for a famous team and earn lots of money. It would guarantee that Ava would have someone who could afford her. How could I tell the love of my life that none of this was going to happen?

Then I just came out with it.

"I'm drafted," I said.

Until that decisive moment, she was so happy. We both were. She gazed into my face. This time her voice was demanding.

"What do you mean?" she asked.

I sat on her sofa and pulled her beside me. Without saying a word, I gave her the letter. She read all of it and paused a long time before she spoke.

"This is all wrong," she said. "Can't you get out of it?

I didn't answer. I got up and started pacing.

"Ken, talk to me! Don't shut me out," she said.

"Say something!"

Her eyes had filled with tears as she looked at me.

I took her back into my arms. I thought if I held her close enough, the pain would stop. She clung to me tightly, but no matter how close I held her, it wasn't close enough. In less than two weeks, I'd not only be her long distance lover, but I'd be a lonely soldier in the United States Army dressed in green with black boots tightly laced above my ankles and a rifle, that I hated the thought of carrying, resting on my shoulder. There were no guarantees I'd ever see her, again.

She started stroking my back.

"We're going to make it," she softly whispered. "I love you. I'll never stop loving you no matter what happens."

She had spoken bravely that night. It was hard to think about leaving as I looked at her, the woman I'd fallen deeply in love with. She was my rock, my bridge— the best thing that had ever happened to me.

"You won't be gone forever," she'd said, squeezing my hand.

I swept her in my arms and kissed her forehead, then her cheeks until I made my way to her lips. I peppered kisses all over her face and pushed aside the tip of her blouse to find her bare shoulders. I buried my head in her hair and inhaled her sweet fragrance as if I could suck all of her inside of me. I felt the power of her love giving way to me. She kissed me back, forcing me to forget the pain for a moment.

"Promise me you'll be here when I get back," I whispered in her ear.

"I'll be right here when you return," she said.

The rest of the evening was spent with us both holding and reassuring each other that we were going to be okay. After an hour, we stopped talking about it.

I had left late that night with her candy sweet kisses still impressed upon my lips and her last words on my mind, reminding me she'd wait for me. A week later, I said goodbye to her and headed to Fort Bragg for basic training. I never imagined she wouldn't be standing in the same place, anxiously waiting to fall into my arms once more.

Tubby's big brown eyes stared at me as if he wanted to console me. My dog then dropped his head between his paws and rested. I patted his head and said goodnight.

The house was quiet when I walked inside. I wasn't sure where my brothers and sisters were, but I was glad they weren't around. I glanced at my mother. She was sitting and folding laundry at the kitchen table. I spoke and rushed to my room. Once inside, I locked the door behind me and fell limp beside my bed.

I thought I was alone in the stillness of the room until I looked up and saw my father at my dresser, digging inside a drawer full of papers.

"What happened back there?" he asked. "Why didn't she bring you home?"

I pulled up onto the edge of the bed and looked over at him. His brow furrowed. Wrinkles that only formed in his forehead when he was perplexed had made deep impressions. I hadn't seen that expression since I was in junior high—when he scolded me for lying about where I'd been.

"We had a fight," I answered in a low breath.

"Did you make her cry?" he asked.

I didn't answer. I knew a lecture was coming. I needed understanding, not a rebuke.

"You made her cry, didn't you?" he demanded.

My father made his way over to my bed and stood there. He looked frustrated. It was seldom I saw him upset. He was a peaceful guy—one who never liked fights or confusion. I'd seen him deal with situations that would make a preacher cuss, but he never said an unkind word. No one quite understood how my father kept his calm composure. But he had his own philosophy about handling situations. "A person can't fight if he's got nobody to fight with," he often said. "Leave the situation alone and it will settle all by itself." He never had much to say. But when he spoke, he left food for thought.

"Son, you don't measure how strong you are by what you say or do," he said. "It's what you could say or do, but decide not to, that shows your strength. What could be so bad that you had to make her cry? That's not how I raised you to treat a woman."

The lecture I dreaded was upon me. He'd ask a question and answer it himself all in one breath. I studied his features. He was a handsome man at forty-five—medium height and lean, brown complexion with deep brown eyes. He was a barber by trade and cut his own hair. I was named after him, and some people said I looked like him, particularly with the distinct curve of my nose showing our ancestral Irish heritage. He was a mixture of African and Irish. My medium brown cheeks held a hint of red hue of Cherokee that I inherited from my mother's side of the family, and a little Irish from my father. All in all, I had African, Indian, and Irish genes—a splendid combination for conversation of inquisitive minds.

I always tried to emulate my father when I was young. He never raised his voice or his hand to me. He drilled in me and my four brothers the idea that a man is supposed to be strong and tough. I never cried or fought back when I was bullied in school until one day I'd had enough and punched the bully. It was the last time he bothered me. My father had no clue as to what happened back there with me and Ava, and I resented his take on what I should've done.

"I heard she was seeing somebody, daddy," I choked.

I pretended not to notice him staring at me. All I wanted was to be left alone. The quicker I was alone to wallow in my sorrow, the better.

My father took in a deep breath. It was a few seconds of silence before he spoke.

"You sure she's going to be all right?" he asked. I gave him a feeble nod. There was a lump in my throat that prevented me from speaking or even crying. And the migraine intensified, sending a blinding pain across my forehead.

My father got up and left my room. I rushed behind him and locked my door. There in the silence, I stretched across my bed and buried my head in my pillow. I was left with my troubled thoughts and questions that only God could answer, and I wasn't sure if I was on his agenda.

I heard my mother's concerned voice searching for answers from my father. "What on earth happened?" I heard her ask.

My father grunted and said, "Girl problems, Mary Rose. These young men have the brains of a fool. They do the craziest things I've ever seen in my life!"

I heard my mother's footsteps stop at my door. She spoke in a soft, faint voice.

"Are you all right, son?"

I didn't answer. My mother was fond of Ava. She was one of the few girls I'd taken home and the only one my mother took a liking to right away. I knew if I told my mother about the argument, she'd reassure me that God was going to work it all out. Everything was about God when it came to my mother.

I could sense she was still standing at my door. I didn't want her kind words. I wanted to be punished for falling in love. I wanted someone to beat me and throw me into the river, leaving me for the sea vultures. I got up and peered through a crack in the door.

"Ava and I broke up," I said. My mother nodded and quietly walked away. I closed the door and crawled back on the bed.

The floor squeaked as her footsteps traveled down the hall. I heard my brothers and sisters moving about throughout the house. Among the eight of us—three girls and five boys, I was the oldest. No one bothered to come in my room. That was to my advantage, because I was a muddle of emotions.

I stayed in a fetal position on my bed and fell asleep. About an hour later, I heard a light tap on my door.

"Bro, it's me," Frank whispered.

If anybody could get me to open the door, my brother, Frank, could. He and I were a lot alike in many ways. I was quiet and reserved at times, and he was the same. And, I could talk to him about anything when I was in the dumps. He'd listen without jokes or judgment.

"I'm coming," I said, as I pulled myself from the covers.

He stood in the door, frowning.

"Are you all right?" he asked.

"I will be," I said.

He sat on the edge of my bed.

"Daddy told me what happened," he said. "I know whatever happened, it wasn't your fault."

I dropped back down on my bed and stared in the ceiling. My mind went to my confrontation with Ava.

"I never thought she would do this," I said. "She promised she'd wait for me."

"I know you feel bad," he said. "But, if she did this to you while you're about to go to war, then maybe she's not the kind of woman you think she is. Better you know, now, than to come back from war and find her with some other guy."

I nodded. There was some truth to what Frank said, but it didn't ease the pain. With my eyes fastened to the ceiling, I began to question my judgment about her. Was this woman—the one I'd pledged my love to for the rest of my life—a fake all along? Did Howard know what kind of girl she was and didn't warn me? I needed answers.

"Wanna ride out?" Frank asked.

"No, I'm good here," I said.

Frank nodded and walked out.

I looked over at the clock. There was still time to go back before she turned in for the night. I wondered what she was doing now. Maybe she called this guy to come over so she could tell him I was finally out of her life. I kept going back to the fact that maybe I should have given her a chance to tell her side of the story. Maybe I had it all wrong.

I jumped up and headed to my bedroom door. Then my mind challenged me. "No, you shouldn't go to her," it warned.

I found a chair in the corner of my room and slumped into it.

An hour later, I had enough of trying to sort things out. I decided to find Howard. I asked my mother if I could borrow her sedan. It was better to ask her rather than my father, I thought. I was afraid he'd offer to drive me and start lecturing again.

My shirt was smelly and damp from perspiration, but I had no strength or will power to shower and change. I hopped in the car and drove downtown to the Two Spot, a juke joint not far from my home. The place was full of tobacco smoke and men and women carousing on the dance floor. R&B music blasted. As soon as I walked in, I saw Howard sitting at a table with his girl, Samantha.

His eyes lit up when he saw me.

"Ken!" he called over the loud music.

He rushed over and gave me a hearty hug. Samantha slid out of her chair and joined him. She wrapped her arms around me and laughed as she patted my midsection.

"Looks like the army is treating you good," she said.

Howard pulled out a chair.

"Sit down and tell us all about basic training," he said.

"Not until Sam gets me something to drink," I replied.

"Sure," Samantha said, as she jumped to her feet.

I watched as she threaded her way through the crowd. As soon as she was out of my sight, I turned to Howard. Before I could speak, he broke in.

"Did they finally make a man out of you? Or you still a mouse?" He laughed and gave me a hard slap on the back. "Man, I can't tell you how good it is to see you!"

He kept on talking, but I didn't hear a word. The place, music, and the people brought back too many memories of me and Ava. The Two Spot is where we first met face to face. I looked at the happy dancers piled in the middle of the floor and envied them.

Someone put on a slow song that brought back more memories of that night—the night I finally got up enough nerve to ask her to dance with me.

I was lost in reverie when Howard gave me a nudge.

"Hey, dude," he said. "Are you listening?"

"Yeah, I heard you," I said.

"So, what time did you get in?" he asked.

"Not long ago," I said.

A tall guy with a beer in one hand and a cigarette in the other came over and struck up a conversation with Howard. Fantastic! It gave me more time to reflect as my eyes traveled about the room.

I looked at the table in the corner where Ava had sat that night. She had been sitting alone when I walked over. The moment was awkward. I didn't know what to do with my hands, so I grabbed the back of a chair. A slow song came on the jukebox. I had stood beside her and shot her a line Howard gave me to strike up a conversation.

"I got the feeling you were waiting for me to come over," I'd said.

I pressed my thigh against the table to keep from shaking. For a man, it's not easy approaching the woman he really likes when he's trying to make a good first impression. I think Ava knew I was a basket of nerves, and she enjoyed teasing me. I noticed a smirk on her face as I stood weak and vulnerable. She remained silent while I waited for a reply. Suddenly, I panicked. It's not working! Howard had warned me that she wouldn't be an easy catch.

I thought to turn and walk away, but instead, I extended my hand.

"May I have this dance?" I asked.

She looked up at me. Then she looked back down at her Coke and started sipping it through a straw. I brought my other hand forward.

"I have this one, too, if you'd like both," I said. Brilliant! I thought. The words flowed without hesitation, and they sounded really good to me. She turned slowly until her entire body was facing me.

"Can you make it worth my time?" she asked with a seductive curve of her lips. She slid out of the chair and threw her shoulders back with an uplifting air of prideful self-assurance and followed me to the dance floor.

Bravo. I'd hit a home run. Although I was standing up on the outside, I was lying prostrate on the inside passed out from shock.

The slow music was still playing. I guided her onto the crowded dance floor. We found a spot that no one had claimed. Her body relaxed, and I pulled her to me until her cheek met mine.

Not being the fondest of the club dance floor, I'd always sit and watch. However, that night was different. It was a few minutes before midnight, and I felt like the prince—center stage with Cinderella. I remembered whispering in her ear. "I would've stood there until the world came to an end."

"I wouldn't have let you," she whispered back. She pulled slightly away and looked into my eyes. She held a soft, loving gaze. Then she shrugged nonchalantly.

"Not that I needed the company," she said. "I just didn't want you standing there looking so stupid."

She threw her head back and giggled. Her humor was odd, and you would have to be careful not to get offended. But it was her liberating, free spirit that caused me to let my guard down and enjoy what I was feeling.

We saw each other every weekend after that night. It wasn't long before our friends started saying we were made for each other. I agreed, but I couldn't figure out why she played so hard to get.

Howard tugged on me, jolting me back. I looked around and the guy he was talking with had left.

"Where are you, man?" Howard asked. "Are you listening to me or not?"

"Huh? What did you say?" I asked, as I tried to pull myself back into the conversation.

"I've been talking my head off," he said. "How have you been?"

I turned to face him. It was more difficult to talk to Howard than I'd thought. I opened my mouth to speak, but I could only whisper.

"I just left Ava's . . ." I said.

It hurt to say her name. I looked through the crowd. To my relief, Samantha was still at the counter. Someone had started a conversation with her.

Howard gave a quick toss of his head toward the door.

"Come on," he said.

He slid out of his chair. Surrounded by the blasting music and thunderous voices, I followed him as he walked outside toward his car. A mournful Howard climbed behind the wheel and motioned for me to get in. Reluctantly, I slid into the passenger's seat. The look on his face told me what he was about to say was not good.

"I didn't want to be the one to write and tell you, but somebody had to," he said.

He lowered his head.

"I saw them everywhere," he said and paused as if he didn't want to say anymore. "They were here at the club, around town . . . everywhere. They never saw me though. I thought she was merely lonely and just needed ordinary company, someone as a friend. But it looked to be more than that. It looked personal."

"Personal?" I asked. "What do you mean?"

"I saw them leave the club one night and followed them out here to the parking lot," he said, as he nodded to a back row of cars parked in dim light. "They did a lot of making out over there."

"Who is he?" I demanded.

"Jerome," Howard said. "I didn't think it would last that long, but . . ."

Howard's voice trailed off as my thoughts spun. My mind was on Jerome. I didn't know him well, but I knew he was a smooth, sleek kind of guy—not anywhere near someone I could see Ava dating. I thought about my going-away party—how I had searched the house and found her in a delightful conversation with Jerome. He moved close—too close for my comfort—and appeared to be whispering something into her ear. I wondered what he said. Perhaps that gesture should've warned me something was up. What a fool I'd been to miss that obvious sign! Later that night, when I mentioned the incident to Howard, he had brushed it off.

"Don't you worry about a thing," he had said. "She's too smart to let that sleeker get to her." I was confident Howard knew what he was talking about.

I leaned my head back on the seat. I had to think. I had to make sense out of what was going on. Why didn't Ava write me and save me the trouble of my finding out through someone else? She owed me that much.

I looked over at Howard. His strained face bore my grief. "What else?" I asked.

"That's all I know about it," he said.

I flung the car door open, jumped out and rushed across the parking lot towards my car. Howard walked rapidly behind me and caught up. He put his hand on my shoulder and spun me around.

"I'm sorry, man," he said. "I should've been watching her better."

"I don't know what's happening to us," I mumbled.

"I can't believe it either," Howard said, shaking his head. "She never appeared to be nothing but happy with you."

"Does Sam know?" I asked.

"I don't think so," Howard said. "She can't hold things long, especially when she's had too much to drink."

I knew Howard was telling me the truth about Samantha. And after a couple of beers, her mouth was a water faucet.

"Look, I'll pick you up tomorrow," Howard offered. "We'll ride out somewhere . . . out of town, to get your head clear."

"No, I got some things to take care of," I said.

Howard's eyes widened.

"Look, whatever you're thinking, it's not worth it." His eyes pleaded. "I know you're hurting. But you don't want to go to back to basic training all messed up."

Though he meant well, Howard's words didn't help. I slid under the wheel of my jalopy and sped off.

CHAPTER 3

I rode for hours around town, wrestling with the thought of going back to Ava's, but I knew Howard was right. Before me was the dreaded battlefield. I had to focus and do everything in my power to keep a level head.

Finally, I drove on home. When I arrived, everybody had gone to bed. I walked into the stillness of the living room and flopped into a chair. My mother always left a low lamplight on when any of us was out after dark. I turned the lamp off and sat listening to the ticking of the wall clock.

When I closed my eyes, Ava's face appeared. I thought about what attracted me to her besides her good looks. She was the first to teach me how to laugh at myself and how not to take life so seriously. She was the only woman I'd gone out with who didn't come with expectations or an agenda. She didn't try to change me. I was a good ole country boy with hardly any sex appeal or charisma, I thought. And, I had no fancy words to impress; just a baseball bat I was good at using. Ava had all the confidence in the world in me when, at times, I doubted myself.

She'd gotten a part of me—a sacred part of my heart that no one else had, and then signed my death certificate. It was so hard to believe I had lost her love, her sweet smile, and the magic of her touch. Surely, she couldn't let what we had stray away like driftwood floating down a river bank.

Suddenly, a car with a loud muffler rattled by, breaking my thoughts. I sat straight up in the chair and looked over at the clock. I'd been sitting about an hour in the dark room, and I still couldn't shut my thoughts off.

My mind shifted to South Vietnam and the war. I thought about how so many of my comrades had left familiar surroundings and loved ones against their wills, and had turned into killing machines. The draft is not a man's dream or a quest to be a heroic patriarch for his country. In fact, it could be a man's worst nightmare. It was certainly mine.

Maybe I missed the government's logic, but I couldn't understand why men who had plans of a bright future should be turned into mass murderers. In my opinion, the real men who needed to go to war were criminals like serial killers on death row. If they enjoyed the sight of blood with no regrets about killing people, then why not draft them? If death is the inevitable for them, why not put them on front line in battle? I was certain my theory would prove favorable to American citizens whose tax dollars accommodated such criminals. One day, I thought, I'd sell my idea to Congress.

Around one o'clock the next morning, I dragged myself to bed and threw myself on top of the covers. I tossed for hours before I fell back asleep.

The following days of my furlough were miserable. I made several attempts to pick up the phone to call Ava, but then I decided against it. Instead, I got busy helping my mother who never stopped finding things for me to do around the house. Occasionally, my brothers and I would ride into town and hang out at a café. In a small town like Lenoir, there wasn't much going on for entertainment.

The week finally came to an end, and it was time for me to leave for AIT and finish my training. Before Howard picked me up around noon and drove me to the bus station, I told my younger sisters and brothers goodbye and made them promise they wouldn't give our parents a hard time. My mother stood beside my father on the porch. Saying goodbye to her was the hardest. She squeezed me tight and said a quick prayer while my father stood next to her.

On the way to the bus station, Howard talked about everything except me and Ava's confrontation. There was absolutely nothing he could've said that would've made me feel better.

It didn't take us long to get to the station, and for once the Greyhound was on time. I bade Howard farewell, step on board and took a window seat. Shortly, I was joined by an elderly woman.

"You look like a kind young man," she said.

I forced a smile back. If only she knew, I thought, that this kind-looking face was a façade; that deep inside the shell was a very troubled and unhappy man.

I arrived in Fort Jackson on a Sunday evening. As was customary, we were called for drills around 4:30 the next morning. It seemed that Quincy, our drill sergeant, could sense the soldier who was missing his girl back home. He was a menace with no apologies. That morning, he leaned over and sang a plaintive tune:

Ain't no use in going home,
Jody's got your girl and gone.

He stood upright and straightened his shoulders with a sardonic smile. His loud, deep voice resounded.

"Sound off!"

We shouted back. "One, two."

"I can't hear you," Quincy yelled. "Sound off."

"Three, four!"

Quincy wasn't tall. He was a wry, lean-looking guy, with a physique that didn't compliment his voice. I often wondered if he specifically trained his voice to baritone so he could sound authoritative.

"Attention!" he called.

We rose spontaneously and began to mark time. Quincy spiritedly walked over to me and started the "Jody" song, again.

Ain't no use in looking back,
Jody's laying in your sack . . .

I had the urge to punch him in the mouth. But of course, rank and position forbade me. I wanted nothing to do with the KP duty, which was the usual punishment for unruly behavior. It was fresh on my mind what happened when I stupidly volunteered for kitchen duties my first week in basic training. My fingers were swollen so badly after peeling potatoes that I couldn't write Ava for an entire week.

Exhausted after our drills, I went straight to my barrack and dived onto my cot, dreading what was ahead—the war in South Vietnam. I thought about the actions of the many young men my age that got drafted, but found a clever way to duck out of it. I wished I'd done the same. From some reports I'd heard, many of them had all kinds of excuses to avoid active service. Some hid behind incompetence during psychological evaluations. Others had the right contact or knew the right people to bail them out. Some even went AWOL. The only men I knew not too bothered by the draft were those that voluntarily enlisted—for whom the allure superseded the terror of combat.

I reached under my pillow and pulled out Ava's picture. I studied the portrait, desperately longing for her.

Travis, my roommate, walked in and saw me gazing at it.

"Is that your girl?" he asked, as he climbed onto his bed on top.

"Yeah . . . was," I said.

Travis reached for the portrait. He stared at it for a couple of seconds, and then he handed it back to me.

"She's a beauty," he said. "Did you say '*was*'?"

"It's a long story," I replied.

"We don't have nothing but time, you know," he said. "Tell me, how you get them to want you in the first place?"

The eager, blue-eyed soldier thought there was something I could teach him. But my last encounter with Ava proved I knew nothing more about women than he did.

Someone called him and he sprang to his feet.

"I'll be right back," he said. "That guy owes me lots of money."

He rushed out of the barrack.

I didn't talk to white guys that often, and I certainly was not up to sharing private information with Travis. He seemed like a nice fellow, but while growing up, I formed an opinion that the white man couldn't be trusted. I'd read stories about Jim Crow and his treatment of slaves. The terrible racial injustice in the South made me wonder why the emancipation took so long in the first place. Blacks were taught to feel inferior, prohibited from education, and forbidden to even as much as look into a white man's face. Under Crow's laws, whites were discouraged from getting too friendly with black people.

In my small mountain town, the white clerks at the supermarkets displayed the most noticeable racial biases. When I'd pay for merchandise, most often, they would wait until I placed the coins on the counter. It was their way of avoiding contact with my hand. I was often overlooked while waiting to be served in places. And more times than I could count, I was referred to as "boy," instead of my name.

Of course, I knew a few decent white folks. My mother was a domestic worker for a white family. This family was good to her and treated our family with kindness. But still, we were in the South. I felt she'd never be anything more than just a wonderful housekeeper.

The barrack was quiet. I pulled out a T-shirt from my duffel bag, and Ava's picture fell out. I didn't know what to do with it. I remembered the joy in her eyes when I slipped the necklace on her and nothing could have been more perfect that night. There was a full moon out without a cloud in the sky. She was in a good mood, and so was I.

"As you know, I'm not rich," I remembered saying. "Right now, I can't buy you pretty things. I don't even have a decent car to drive you around town. But I give you my heart . . . and this." I pulled out the necklace. It was a pendant in the shape of a heart with diamonds all around. I saved up all of the money from my part-time job to get it.

Her eyes widened when she saw it. And then I asked her to go steady with me. For a moment, the only movement was her eyes dancing from the necklace to me, and then she burst into laughter.

"I love you!" she said.

She wrapped her arms around me and hugged me so tightly that it almost took my breath away.

I took her by the hand and went outside. We sat on the steps of the front porch, snuggled and kissed. She kept giggling and thanking me for making her birthday special. It was a perfect night.

I stretched out on my bed and thought about how quickly my life had changed from immeasurably happiness to despair. I kept telling myself that Ava would see her mistake with Jerome in the next week or so.

"I don't want any other man," she'd said, before I left for training. "I see what I want in front of me."

That had settled everything for me. I would've gone that day and got her to the nearest altar as fast as I possibly could, if she'd been willing.

Travis returned to the barrack. He hurried over to me with a smile on his face.

"I got my money," he said, holding several twenty dollar bills up. "We had a bet and I won," he added.

I placed Ava's picture back in my jacket pocket.

"That must make you feel on top of the world," I said.

"Yeah, he didn't believe me when I told him I'd been playing poker since I was five," Travis said, smiling big. "But he kept raising the bet. Well, who came out on top?"

He laughed and then hopped on his bunk.

"Now, you were talking about your girl. I'm all ears," he said.

"Don't feel up to talking about it now," I said.

I averted eye contact with him and crawled in bed.

About a week before finishing AIT, the news spread throughout base that our nation's great civil rights leader, Dr. Martin Luther King, Jr., had been assassinated. For a moment, I was speechless. It seemed like a horrible nightmare. Discussions of the assassination dominated the day.

I watched some white guys huddle together in the mess hall. A few sat at my table, but when I was joined by a couple of my black brothers and we started talking about King's death, they acted uncomfortably and left. At first, I didn't know what to make of their hesitancy to join us in our conversation. After all, it was a devastating situation that should have affected all Americans and provoked serious conversations.

Finally, one white soldier with a large tattoo of a squirrel on his left arm approached me and three other black brothers.

"He was a great leader and didn't deserve this," he said.

I looked in his face and saw he was sincere. A few other white men overheard. They looked our way and then huddled back together and whispered something that was inaudible.

"I feel the way you do," I said to the tattooed soldier.

That's all I could say. I appreciated his genuineness, but it was hard to believe he understood my feelings. I saw Travis interacting with some black soldiers. He tried to strike up a conversation with one of them. There wasn't anything wrong with his approach, just the timing. The soldier got up, walked away without saying a word, and joined some other black comrades across the room. I wasn't holding anything personally against Travis, so I went over to him.

"Look, we as a people are in a terrible place right now," I tried to explain. "Give us time to get adjusted to this news."

He lit a cigarette and nodded. I could tell by the expression on his face that he really didn't understand how we felt. He didn't understand that our hero—a man who had dared to stand in the face of injustice and fight for the civil rights of an oppressed people—was dead.

Tensions rose across the room. I overheard a testy conversation between a black soldier and two white soldiers.

"There's no way in the hell we can keep letting this shit happen," the black soldier said, as he chewed on a candy bar.

One white soldier who looked frustrated answered back. He had a slight stutter.

"A lot of us white people oppose the horrible things done to blacks," he said. "You can't blame all of us."

"That's right," another white guy said in support.

The tall, black soldier looked at them with fire in his eyes. "Hell, there are many of your kind, not necessarily belonging to the Klan, who believe since the voting rights was passed that it should be enough for us. That's a lot of bullshit if you ask me. They didn't do us a favor."

I stepped outside for fresh air. I felt sorry for our white comrades. Their ignorance was justified. They'd never walked in a black man's shoes. They'd never been handed food through a hole in a window at a restaurant; they never had to use dirty toilets meant for blacks only; they'd never seen the deep, dark scars on their grandfathers' back from slave owners' whips; or watch their mother's eyes fill with tears as people tried to explain how her boy died hanging from a tree. Where does America go from here? And how many more blacks would die before the freedom bell rings? I thought to myself.

I tried to push King's death out of my head. The best I could do was to keep my mind on the fight in the jungles of South Vietnam and hope I'd live to see Ava again.

CHAPTER 4

It was a clear day in late May, 1968, when I finished my eight weeks of AIT in South Carolina. Only Howard was there for the ceremony. I asked him to come. I didn't pressure my family to attend, because it wasn't a celebration I was happy about. It only meant one thing to me. Soon, I would join my comrades against the hardcore Viet Cong.

On a refreshingly cool day in April, about one hundred of Company D stood in perfect formation on a field behind the barracks.

A large crowd had gathered. I wasn't there mentally. I had never thought of it before, but that day, I contemplated going AWOL. I planned how I would go about it. I'd wait until we were in California heading to South Vietnam, and then I'd find a way to get lost from my unit. I pondered that thought until I heard the crowd applauding as the CO took his position at the podium.

During his lengthy oration, thoughts of Ava bombarded my mind. A plane appeared in the distance. It reminded me of my daydream for us. I wanted to take her on a private jet to some island. I'd read about a guy flying his girl on a private plane to Aruba for Christmas. I knew it seemed unlikely it would happen, now that I was going to war. Nevertheless, I saw no harm in daydreaming about the enchanting island

and its white sandy beaches. It was a perfect dream, I thought, even though it may never come true.

The commander's voice escalated.

"And in addition," he said. "These men have demonstrated commitment and dedication to this country through their training both at basic and here in AIT. And have successfully completed basic training. They have shown discipline and devotion to accomplish a mission set before them. It is our country's . . ."

His speech trailed off. In my head, I heard Ava's voice saying, "I'll be right here when you return." It would be a long time before we could be together, but she knew that. And if she was afraid I would not return alive, then that made two of us.

My eyes shifted to the sky. I watched the plane until it was buried behind a few scattered clouds. The commander had his final words.

"In spite of the hazards inherit," he said. "They are willing to fight valiantly for the cause of democracy. I proudly honor these men with the official title, Private First Class."

He saluted the sergeant next to him and allowed him to take over.

"Attention . . . fall out!" the sergeant said.

A loud applause erupted from the bleachers. I shook my legs and arms to get proper circulation flowing. We had been locked at attention for about an hour.

Travis put his hand on my shoulder.

"I guess this is it," he said. "We weren't the lucky ones to get the same orders. Maybe we will hook up somewhere after this is over."

I turned and looked into his face. "Have you ever loved a woman so hard that it hurts to breathe?" I asked.

Travis looked confused and shook his head.

"The pain digs its way through every cell in your body. It's killing you inch by inch," I continued. "And somewhere in the back of your mind, you think if you let go, your whole life would go, too."

Travis frowned, and then he chuckled.

"She must be some kinda woman," he said.

"Never fall in love," I said. "It hurts like hell and it might just kill you."

Travis left with a bewildered look on his face. Howard had overheard our conversation. He walked up behind me.

"What kind of stupid advice was that?" he asked. "Did you see the look on his face? You scared the hell out of him."

"Great," I said. "Now, come on. I'm hungry."

Howard walked alongside and threw his arm around my shoulder.

"I'm proud of you, man," he said.

I stopped and turned to him.

"Look, I want you to write me only if Ava has a change of heart about us," I said. "Don't write me until then, okay?"

"That's crazy," he said. "I thought we're going to stay in touch."

"Ask my mother," I said. "She'll let you know how I'm doing."

I grabbed his shoulder and made him look me in my eyes.

"Promise me you will not write unless there's good news about Ava," I said. "That she wants to apologize and she wants me back."

Howard dropped his head. "Do not write unless there's good news," I said. "Is that clear?"

"Look, I don't mean to pour vinegar on your wound," Howard said. "But my God, man! Why are you trying to hold on?"

He stopped when he saw the disdained look on my face.

"Okay, okay," he said, throwing up both of his hands. "I just want you to stop and think about what happened here. You didn't break up with her. She's the one who messed around."

"I didn't give her a chance to talk to me," I said. "I should've gone back over there and heard her out. There's got to be a good excuse for why she didn't wait for me. Who knows, Jerome could've taken advantage of her vulnerable moment or something."

A sharp pain crossed my midsection when I said that. I couldn't bear to think about it.

"I know when she has time to think about us, she'll change her mind," I said. "Women do that, you know. Remember when you and Samantha were about to split? She thought about it, right? And now you both are back together."

"Yeah, I hear you," Howard said.

"So . . . when do you write me?" I looked squarely at him. He sighed, shaking his head. When he saw I wasn't changing my mind, he gave in.

"Only when Ava and Jerome have split," Howard said.

I was satisfied. I could count on him doing what I asked of him. It might have sounded ridiculous to him. But if Ava never wrote as I felt she would, Howard's letter would be my hope—telling me that she's done with Jerome and wants to reconcile with me.

I looked around the grounds of the place that had been my home. Strangely, I dreaded leaving the camp, even though basic training was murder on my body. I'd had enough push-ups, climbing fences and jumping hurdles to pull a tracker-trailer out of a ditch. Some mornings were bitterly cold. Between basic and AIT training, we ran in rain, sleet and snow with temperatures near freezing. Nonetheless, it was home where I felt safe.

My mind turned to Vietnam. With only a few days left, I would leave the wonderful states of America to join my fellow comrades in a war that up until then, I had only read about or seen on the news.

It was as though Howard read my mind. He slapped me on my back.

"You're going to be fine," he said.

We left the field and headed out to find a restaurant. Howard spent most of the time trying to encourage me for the fight ahead. I hardly listened. I knew he meant well, but all I wanted was to be left alone.

That night, I took a good look at the man in the mirror. Fatigue showed in the crevices of my cheeks. I didn't sleep at all the night before. I had tossed in my sleep all night, waking two or three times before morning. There were noticeable bags under my eyes. My skin looked dull. It lacked the luster it once held. The heartache of losing Ava was not taking a back seat and realization of the formidable task in the jungles was settling on me.

I stared at my uniform that Ava loved to see me wear. Now, it felt like a mourner's attire. I was no longer the soldier and the lover that made her so proud. I was simply an ordinary man in uniform.

At the end of the week, my unit arrived in Charlotte, North Carolina. With duffel bags on our backs, a busload of us boarded a plane for Oakland, California.

Before landing, you could see the busy port and shipyards. Oakland's fertile flatland soils made the city's landscaping rich and vibrant.

We stepped out of the terminal under the clear skies. It was eighty degrees. We had a bite to eat and then turned in for the evening.

I took in everything of the small room where I'd stay overnight—the smell of clean, fresh sheets, fresh towels, the nice fragrance of bath soap, including the feel of the shower's warm water splashing on my back. They were luxuries that would soon be a memory.

We sat on the runway at Oakland airport on a sunny morning. I was told we'd leave there and travel twenty-two hours, having one layover in Guam before leaving for Saigon.

I had no way of knowing if Howard had talked with Ava, yet. However, I was sure he'd keep his word and write. I kept beating myself up over the fact that I didn't let her tell me what happened. Her explanation might have saved us. Another thought crossed my mind that nearly caused me to panic. What if he asked her to marry him? I couldn't handle that thought, so I pulled out a magazine to read.

A couple of the soldiers sitting in the mid-section of the plane started singing a song by R&B singer, Jerry Butler. I joined them in the chorus. "Only the strong survive. Only the strong survive. You better be strong, you better hold on," I sang loudly.

None of us could recall all of the lyrics, but what we could remember was appropriate for what we were going to face. Dreading the grueling task in front of me, I closed my eyes while the lyrics played over and over in my head, "You better be strong, you better hold on."

There was a lot of joking among the guys about the army making men out of us. One guy, looking to be about twenty-five, laughed and said, "If they needed to find out if I'm a man or not, they should've asked my wife. She had a nice smile on her face when I turned over."

A roar of laughter came from the men. It was the lower part of their anatomy and women that created the most conversation.

The pilot announced take off. I stared out of the window while my mind raced ahead. After about twelve flight hours, I would no longer look down over American soil but the jungles of South Vietnam. I felt alone. I looked at the soldiers—some sleeping and others were staring into space. I wondered if they were in as much anguish about their uncertain future as I was.

The plane taxied the runway and finally lifted into the clear blue skies. A soldier next to me was looking through a small photo album. I didn't think to bring any pictures other than the ones of Ava. A lot of picture taking occurred at my going-away party, but in every photo of the two of us, I wore a stone face. I never wanted the party in the first place, but when I protested, she rationalized it by saying people who loved me wanted to see me and wish me well. "You owe them that much," she said. I begged to differ.

I gave in to her desire to have the party, but I couldn't fake what I was feeling that night. It had not been ten minutes after the first guest arrived when I got restless. I couldn't stand in one spot and talk with anyone for more than a couple of minutes without excusing myself.

Ava had invited lots of her friends—some I didn't know at all. I think some of them came to pity me—the poor soldier who happened to get picked out of hundreds. Perhaps I was a coward … afraid of the war. Who could fault me? The grim reports of South Vietnam were on the evening news, including headlined newspapers and magazine stands everywhere in town. In my opinion, the number of fallen men was higher than they were reporting.

That night, I watched a couple that seemed to be madly in love—holding hands and looking into each other's eyes the way Ava and I did when we were together. My eyes shifted to the other men in the room with their sweethearts. After the party, they would go home, snuggle and go on with their lives. My life had stopped. What had I done to deserve this? Was an omen hanging over me?

I stepped away into the hall, walked into the kitchen and poured a glass of punch. The laughter grew louder. I listened to the merriment with envy.

I looked across the room at one of the men who'd gotten a draft letter the same day I'd gotten mine. He was joking and clowning around as if nothing crucial had happened. It must be the spiked punch, I thought to myself. Perhaps he was trying to drown his sorrows, too.

Everybody was having a wonderful time, all but me.

Many people had greeted me and then headed straight for the refreshments. Not one soul thought to ask how I was feeling. I'd soon be a soldier joining my fellow comrades in a god-forbidden war, in a country I knew nothing about; leaving behind the only woman I loved and nobody seemed to care.

Later that night, Ava and I slipped away from the party. The people were having such a good time that no one even noticed we were leaving.

My passion was burning. I wanted to light up the night in the backseat of my Ford. To my surprise, all she wanted to do was talk. Sometimes women find the most inopportune time to share their deepest thoughts. We got up and sat on her front porch in an old wooden swing that squeaked. She talked about how she couldn't sleep, because she was thinking about us. She was concerned about my going to Vietnam to fight. She wanted to know what would happen to us if I stayed longer than my DEROS. Now that I look back, I'm sure something was going on in her head. She wanted to tell me, and I missed it altogether.

After our layover in Quam, I slept most of the trip to Saigon. I woke when I heard the pilot announcing touchdown. Through the window, I could see the city. It was lovely with its carefully crafted architectural buildings and its exotic wildlife. I was taken aback. I had a distorted picture of the country. With only the images from the evening news of the war, I imagined the entire city in shambles.

Once we landed on the foreign soil, about twenty of us PFC soldiers changed planes in Saigon and quickly boarded a chopper headed for our 1st Division base camp.

I gazed down onto the country comprised of highlands, rainforests, and graciously blessed fertile deltas. The indescribable vibrant green land was breathtaking.

When we got closer to our base camp, the scenery changed. My stomach tightened. There was a huge area where rockets had landed. The hollow mass of destruction had claimed the home of the wildlife, leaving nothing to my imagination. The few times I'd watched the reports of the war on the evening news, it was nothing close to what we were experiencing. It was ten times worse. The cruel battle between the communist North and non-communist South had transformed the lovely verdant mountains and lively green forest into a black sweltering pot.

We arrived in a place called Dion which was one of our base camps. I would be assigned to company, D 1/28 battalion known as the Black Lions.

The chopper descended, sending wildlife below rushing for cover. We landed in a clear area. One by one, our strapped boots hit the ground. A heat wave struck us with temperatures as high as 110 degrees—a drastic change from the mild temps we'd left in the states. There were a few scattered clouds, but they offered no relief from the blazing sun.

I grabbed my duffel bag and walked rapidly behind the other men toward our camp. The stench was horrible. It smelled like sewage, only twice as bad. A sharp pain swept across my forehead from the scorching sun, and sweat poured profusely under my shirt.

Finally, we arrived at headquarters. In front of us was a sign over the entrance that read:

NO MISSION TOO DIFFICULT, NO SACRIFICE TOO GREAT
DUTY FIRST

I gazed at the sign with an overwhelming feeling of helplessness. It was then that I knew my life was about to drastically change. We were in the death trap, as I called it. The dense jungles of South Vietnam and its deep rice patty fields and ravaged valleys were before us.

I followed the other men in my unit inside the headquarters. We sat down and waited. I glanced at one of the men who sat next to me. He was smiling while reading a letter. I couldn't help but think it was from his wife or sweetheart. I envied him. I thought about Ava and wondered if she was thinking about me at all? Did she miss me even for a second?

The voices of several men broke into my thoughts. I looked up into the faces of three black soldiers and two white. They walked over and greeted us with handshakes. Some of them were leaving for home. They were jubilant and full of jokes.

One black soldier, dark complexion with a gap between his teeth, walked around and patted all ten of us one by one on our shoulders.

"Welcome Long Timers to the Big Red One," he said with a chuckle. "You'll learn to love it here."

The soldier who made that remark was a short-timer, meaning he was on his way back to the states. I guess he found some humor in his greeting. As a new arrival on that day, I found his welcome to be in poor taste.

There were no smiles or laughter from those of us who'd gathered that afternoon for our instructions. We sat quietly like first graders while our CO marched from side to side with a hard look on his face. He was a medium-built man with a salt and pepper mustache and splashes of gray around the edges of his hairline. He wore a noticeable scar on the side of his face. He pointed to it.

"There are other scars like this that you can't see," he said. He then put his hand over his heart. "Right here when my men didn't return from battle—responsible brave men who'd fought valiantly and died in honor with letters from home that were never opened."

The officer's voice rang out loudly and firmly as though he knew our thoughts. He didn't spare our inhibitions and fears, but went on to say, "Some of you will die, some will be wounded, and some of you will return and live."

My heart almost stopped when he said that. I recalled my mother's words the day I found out about my draft. "You'll be wounded," she'd said. The captain had spoken her words. An eerie feeling crept over me.

"This is where you'll apply the training you've learned," he went on to say. "You're very capable of fighting this battle. I expect a great work from all of you."

He paused for a moment and then, for whatever reason, he walked up to me.

"Private First Class, do you hear me?" His white cheeks flushed red as he stared into my face.

"Yes, sir!" I answered with my shoulders squared and eyes locked on the wall ahead of me. He stood a few seconds, and then started to pace in front of us.

"Trust no one," he said. "These damn gooks are smart. They could look like anyone of the villagers. If you gotta crap or piss in the bushes, call for someone to cover your ass. No one needs to get shot over your shit."

He then stopped pacing. In a strong, yet fatherly voice, he said, "You are committed to the mission set before us. You are trained and ready for the task ahead. Keep alert at all times. And good luck, men."

When he walked away, a sudden unexpected zeal came upon me. It was strange, but I felt extremely anxious to get to the battlefield. I had pent up frustrations and needed somewhere to put them. I was "gung ho" and rushed after my commander and stopped him.

"Sir," I said.

He turned around. I stood looking straight into his eyes.

"Sir, when is the first fight, sir?"

"The time will come soon enough, soldier," he said, and shook his head. Walking away, he called over his shoulder. "Basic training only prepares you, G.I. . . . it won't save you."

That evening, I sat with a group of my black brothers in the mess hall and ate my first meal—buffalo meat, tossed salad consisting mostly of lettuce, and the usual potatoes. No matter what, a military meal always consisted of potatoes.

As I gulped down a mouthful, a tall, stocky black soldier with huge hands walked in. He stood about 6'4" with broad shoulders. He had thick arms like a bodybuilder. He looked much like the actor, Forest Whitaker, with no real expression of any kind when he approached me.

"You think you're ready for the fight, soldier?" he asked.

I nodded.

"I heard you're ready to go kill some Cong," he said, chuckling a little.

At first, I didn't know why he'd singled me out. Then it occurred to me that he had possibly spoken with my CO, who told him about the question I'd asked. I answered him, repeating my CO's words.

"The time will come soon enough," I said.

I observed the big fellow as he sat down. He looked bold and confident, traits I was missing. He crossed his legs and got comfortable beside me.

"Name's George Dowd," he said. "Everybody calls me Big Daddy." He extended his hand. "I'm your squad leader."

"Pleased to meet you," I said. I returned his firm handshake. "Ken Dula, from North Carolina."

"We like 'em like you," Big Daddy said. "Gotta have guts out here. No time to think about home. It won't be too hard to get adjusted. Just keep your head on straight."

He introduced me to a platoon leader—a tall, sturdy white soldier with a cigarette hanging loosely in the corner of his mouth.

"Carolina, this is Sergeant Dan Brody," Big Daddy said. It was a habit for military soldiers to call each other by their home state. Big Daddy turned to Brody. "He's a mama's boy. I betcha she named him 'Kenny Boy'."

Both men laughed. My face was stone. I'd lost the woman of my life. I'd been forced into a place I feared the most. Torturing thoughts of dying never left me, and I hated mama jokes. Where was the humor?

Big Daddy had a strange disposition that I didn't get right away. He was humorous, but at the same time, he seemed serious-minded and unapologetic.

Brody shook my hand. He talked fast, telling me that he knew some people from my state. "I'm from Ohio," he said. "I like North Carolina. I tried talking my parents into moving there. It's a great state."

"Yeah . . . good old mountaineer living," I said.

Brody's eyebrows rose. "Are you from Appalachian?"

"Not far," I said.

"Well, whadda you know?" Brody said. "I got some friends near you." He took a cigarette out and handed me the pack.

"There's a welcome gift in there," he said, smiling as he walked away with Big Daddy.

The tobacco pack was a pleasing sight. I never smoked until I got into basic training. Afterwards, I smoked more than I should have, but it was the only thing I had that relaxed me.

I pulled out a Marlboro from the pack and noticed an unusual stem inside. I sniffed the tightly rolled brown wrapper and gasped. Leaping up, I searched for Brody. I never smoked pot before, and I wasn't about to experiment at this point, I thought. I'd heard some of my friends talking about their first high off a joint, but it wasn't something I was anxious to try.

Brody had disappeared like a ghost. I pulled out all of the Marlboro cigarettes and stuffed them into my shirt pocket. The pungent smell of marijuana lingered in my nose even when I walked away, leaving the twisted stem in the pack on the table. I figured some eager soul would find it and make good use of it.

I moved across the room and joined three other men who were in a poker game. They told tales about how they left their women in bed begging for more. We all knew the tales were made-up and full of deception, but it sounded good. Laughter spilled, but I couldn't join them. There was nothing funny to me.

Before long, the conversation turned grim. The short-timers started telling us about the horrible situation in Vietnam. There was one soldier who'd been in the country nearly two years. He talked more than the others about what was ahead. The Vietnamese soldiers were launching what was known as the TET Offensive, the turning point of the war where the Viet Cong prepared for major offensives against our forces. It meant the North Vietnamese aggression was all over the country. It would be one of the worst fought battles we would encounter.

"Expect high casualties," he said.

I looked at the faces of the men who'd traveled with me and wondered if we all were thinking the same thing. Which one of us would be returning home in the wooden box?

CHAPTER 5

That night, next to my cot, a soldier sat writing a letter. My eyes fell on the first two lines he had written: "We have arrived. It's hot as hell and smells like it, too." It was a weird way to start a letter. But I wholeheartedly agreed with his observations.

I pulled out a stack of letters that Ava had written while I was in basic training and opened one and read it over and over.

My, God! I missed her. I was lost without her.

I walked outside to be alone. It was a full moon hanging overhead that brought back memories of the first time I'd made love to Ava. It was a wonderful night at Lovers Cove, a deserted dirt road leading to an abandoned farm about a mile from the main highway. Every couple in high school went to that spot.

On both sides of the road, there was a stretch of thick cedars, creating the perfect setting for romance. Someone said the place got its name because of a newly wedded couple that got lost on the way to the lake. The two stopped there for the night, and the family who owned the farm put them up. Having discovered its romantic charm, the couple fell in love with the place and bought the entire farm. The two lovers grew old together and later died.

It was an indulging story, whether it was true or not. And when you sat in your car on a moonlight night, it was as if you were that couple—lost in time, away from all the cares of the world.

We were alone at Lovers Cove that late evening, which was unusual. Everybody in town was talking about going to the Two Spot to see a popular rock 'n roll band out of Hickory, North Carolina. It suited me just fine. Ava and I were alone together, uninterrupted by flashing headlights of other lovers trying to get a good spot to make out.

Up until then, I hadn't gone any further than kissing her along with a little petting on the sofa at her apartment. I wasn't about to risk making out there. I wanted her badly, but I didn't know how far I should go. Most of the women I'd dated thought that men wanted only one thing from them—sex. I wasn't that kind of guy, and I didn't want her getting misconceptions about me. However, seeing her under the sky filled with the full moon over us made it impossible to keep my hands off of her that night.

I pulled her in my arms and planted a soft kiss on her lips. I could feel her body give way as she pressed closer. I couldn't wait any longer. I opened the car door, rushed around to her side and helped her into the back seat. My heart raced and my knees weakened as I anticipated what was about to happen.

Without any coercing on my part, she stretched out. Her leg fell to one side. I looked into her eyes and saw longing, love, and contentment. I slid on top. She smiled, allowing my hands to travel the curve of her hips.

"I love you so much," I whispered.

"I love you, too," she whispered back. "Hold me."

I squeezed her, pulling her closer to me. She melted in my arms and started returning my kisses with much more passion at times than

I was giving. That was when I was sure we both wanted it. She never said I was her first, but it didn't really matter. Her love was all I wanted

I felt her heart pounding, each beat after mine. I wasn't dreaming. She was there—buried in my arms, my heart and soul. Her blouse was partially open as if her breast had extended an invitation to me. I ran my finger down her cleavage and unbuttoned her shirt. She wore a white lace bra that locked in the front. I reached to unsnap it, but she had already done so. Perhaps, I'd been too cautious, I thought. Maybe she'd been waiting for this moment as much as I'd been.

Her breath was in my ear as she made a slight whimper. I buried kisses in her soft locks of hair, then to her cheeks and finally finding her lips. She moved underneath as I slipped out of my shirt. I looked down on her. Her eyes were closed, waiting for my touch. Carefully, I removed her blouse like an artist unwrapping an expensive painting. Under the moonlight, her skin radiated with a magnificent glow. I caressed her, gently moving my fingers over parts of her body where she'd given permission. She pressed her fingers into my back, placing heavy, panting kisses on my chest.

"You are everything I ever wanted," she whispered.

I'll never forget the look in her eyes when she said that. We took our time that glorious night, allowing our love to find its path to ecstasy, rendering us helplessly lost in its power.

The soldier put his letter down and turned to me.

"It's about chow time," he said.

I stuffed Ava's letter in my shirt and followed him to supper.

Three days later, we received orders for our first mission to sweep Thunder 13. That was the name given to the long hot journey in search of mines. There were thirteen miles of dangerous grounds to cover. The battlefield was inevitable, and the orders were given clearly and precisely.

The morning came quickly. We sat listening at Big Daddy's instructions as he described the conditions.

"We're going into unfriendly territory," he said. "Everything you've heard about this damn war so far, believe it."

He walked back and forth talking with his hands.

"The village people are helpful and happy to see us. However, don't take a damn thing for granted. Some of the young tribesmen may be your worst nightmare. They dress like civilians . . . in pajama pants, carrying baskets that may be full of explosives." He paused and looked into our faces. "You know your mission—search, kill, and destroy. The villagers are very familiar with the jungle. We foreigners are not." He paused and took in a deep breath.

"Use both sets of eyes," he said. That was a term used meaning we had to cover our comrades while looking out for ourselves.

Someone coughed and I jumped. I was afraid of living and dying. I feared living because of illusions and wild imaginations I couldn't control. I had heard stories of soldiers losing their limbs, or becoming so mentally incapacitated that they would never return to a life of normalcy. I feared dying because of the unknown. I wondered about the afterlife, not sure if I would end up in heaven or hell.

I climbed into the chopper with the men in my unit. Packed like chickens in a crate, we headed for our area of operation.

I fumbled in my jacket to check for Ava's picture.

"Forget about Ava," were Howard's words. "She's moved on." I don't think he understood how hopelessly lost I was without her. I was certain Ava would think about what she'd done and that she would give us another try. After we landed, we walked for several miles as we moved slowly toward the village. The villagers seemed to have adjusted to the war regardless of the sounds of rockets and bombs falling only a short distance away. I stared at the dirty pathways of blood where the dead had been dragged and wondered how these people could carry on their day to day living as if nothing happened.

I was appointed as point man—one of the most dangerous positions assigned to a soldier. Every soldier had that assignment at some point.

I held my rifle firmly and stepped cautiously. I was keenly aware of carefully placed mines—ones that could blow a body several feet into the air or ones large enough to sink a tank. We didn't know where our enemy was crouching.

As we drew closer to where we'd set up our ambush, I saw movement. Big Daddy saw my signal and called out, "Cover!" His voice roared like a thousand thunders. Without warning, we were met with sniper fire.

Instantly, my captain's words came to mind. "It would come soon enough." My hands got clammy. Heat rushed up the back of my neck. It would be my first time using my gun in combat. I fired repeatedly, pressing forward with my squad.

We pushed the enemy farther into the jungle. It was hard to tell how many were out there. Keeping low, I crawled on my knees and fired toward the enemy positions. Suddenly, a Viet Cong appeared out of nowhere. I froze for a second. Luckily, I spotted him first and fired upon him, dropping him to his knees. My stomach turned and I felt sick all over.

The Viet Cong didn't give up easily. We were pinned down for several hours. It was just like Big Daddy and our CO had told us. At times, it was difficult to tell the enemy from the civilians.

The irony of it all, the Viet Cong were not well-educated fighters. We were told most of their leaders were men who learned to fight merely by survival trade. Unlike American soldiers, the Viet Cong never had training in ROTC schools or sixteen weeks of intense workouts. Some of them had no more than a six or seventh grade education, yet they demonstrated great artistic skills in combat. They made weapons out of anything—cans, dud rounds, or any material they could get their hands on. They could fight, and they fought hard.

We radioed for support and continued to pound the enemy. In a matter of minutes, we saw our cobra gunships coming to cover our flanks. It was a welcomed sight. Clusters dropped to clear the area. Fire gushed upward and spread rapidly through the bush.

I looked around at the troubled faces of my comrades who were new to the war like me and wondered if they felt the same as I did after killing their first human being. It wasn't fun looking in the face of a man with no other alternative but to shoot him. I felt sick to my stomach. I looked at my hands. They were still trembling long after I fired my first shot. While I sat with my head lowered, Brody leaned over to me.

"This is your first fight, right?" he asked.

I nodded.

His face was hard and stern. "The first time I shot a gook, I had that same look on my face," he said. "After a while, it'll feel the same as if you'd shot a wild jungle cat. You'll just do your job without thinking."

I supposed he said that to make me feel better, but it didn't. I was disturbed by the merciless look on his face and lack of emotions. Sooner or later, I thought, the impact of the war would turn me into that same kind of soldier. I feared that more than the war, itself.

That day, after about eight hours of searching for the enemy and fighting in Thunder 13, we climbed aboard the chopper and headed back to camp. I was still shaking like I'd had a bad neurological reaction to some nerve gas. I looked over at one of my comrades. He kept his head buried in his hands, and he didn't say a word.

I looked down onto the area we'd blasted. It was hard to tell the body count of the enemy, but the thing I knew for certain, I wasn't dreaming. I'd just had my first encounter in the cruel act of war, and it wasn't anything to write home and brag about.

The loud roar of the chopper drowned out the thoughts in my head. I closed my eyes and listened to the engine. It sounded like multiple thunder bursts clustered together.

Finally, we arrived at base. Once we settled in, we got the good news that there were no casualties and none wounded. After being accounted for, we headed straight for the NCO club on base. Everyone had the same thing on their mind— getting to the bar. I squeezed in between Big Daddy and another soldier who looked like he'd been drinking for hours.

"That was too close for comfort," I said to Big Daddy.

He nodded as he held a beer bottle tightly between his fingers. "Yeah, Carolina," he said. "One thing's for sure you're not in a movie. This is the real deal."

"How many do you think were out there?" I asked.

Brody overheard and spoke up.

"Hell, it felt like 'bout a hundred of them sons-of-bitches!" He pulled out a cigarette and lit it. "And that's no joke."

I watched as he took a deep draw of tobacco. He started boasting aloud about how well he could use his gun. He then went on to say how he had a sixth sense and could tell exactly when the enemy would strike. Big Daddy and I exchanged glances. We knew he had diarrhea of the mouth, and he knew nothing at all about the enemy's position or how many he'd shot single-handedly. But, to appease him, we listened with feeble nods.

As the week wore on, I tried to put behind what had happened in the field in order to prepare mentally for the next mission ahead of us.

Late one evening, I looked up and saw a chopper flying into base to deliver mail. We all rushed about, trying to be the first to get to it. I grabbed my stack of mail and hurried to find a quiet place to see if there was a letter from Howard with news that Ava and Jerome had split.

We didn't get mail often, but when it caught up with us, sometimes I'd have three or four letters from my mother. I was glad when that happened, because to the other men, it looked like I had a lot of people writing to me.

Quickly, I thumbed through the pile of envelopes. My heart sank. There was nothing from Howard. For several minutes, I sat looking at the other soldiers smiling and some reading out loud. A moment later, I gathered my mail and went outside. There was a quiet wind blowing. It all reminded me of the many times Ava and I spent at the lake.

My mind went to our first kiss as I held her in my arms that night and prayed God would hold time with her a little longer—a lot longer, forever longer.

I stopped daydreaming and fished back through the stack of mail. There were two letters from my mother and one from my hometown buddy who'd just finished Barber College. We had graduated together, so the talk about barbering was refreshing.

I pulled a letter from the three my mother had written. She told me that my father had come down with the flu, and he was bedridden. I mused at that thought. My father never liked being confined to the house. I could imagine how upset he was when he couldn't get out and drive his Rambler.

I read on, and then I got to some shocking news. My mother mentioned the death of my cousin. He was innocently walking along the road when two white men rode up. According to witnesses, one of the men yelled "nigger" at my cousin. Moments later, the driver ran him over and sped off, dragging him about fifty feet. My cousin died instantly.

Distraught, I put the letter down. It took a moment before I could open any more mail. Even though several months had passed since Dr. King's assassination, from the reports we were getting, there was still unrest all over the South. Before my cousin's death, I sat with several black brothers who said they'd gotten letters from home telling them about their relatives in the rural areas of Alabama, Mississippi, and Georgia. During the protests in the heat of racial conflict, they had lost their homes. Their neighborhoods were burned down, and other despicable acts of racism were all over their cities. There were reports of friends who had their cars smashed and their children mocked in school. In Alabama, particularly, men and women were beaten on sidewalks as they were walking home or attempting to catch the bus.

I listened to their stories, never once thinking one of my family members would become a victim of racial violence. I got plenty worried about my folks back home. The small, rural mountain town of Lenoir had never experienced any open brutality of that magnitude. By no means were blacks in my hometown treated well. They just didn't speak out much about the injustice. Our schools had begun integrating in 1965, and people of both races were disturbed about it. There were subtle hints in the newspaper columns, and I would overhear white folks' conversation in coffee shops about their uneasiness with integration. But, all in all, there were never any blatant signs of hatred toward us blacks, just pure ignorance.

I sat down on the ground for about an hour with thoughts about my cousin's death and the war, itself. As a black American draftee, I found it difficult to understand it all. I was fighting a war in South Vietnam that made no sense to me. While I was serving my country, my black race was being ridiculed, beaten and tortured back home. I was glad I was a United States' citizen. But the history of my heritage, my ancestors' struggles during slavery, and our current ongoing fight for racial equality in America was of the upmost concern to me, especially while the danger grew in my own home town.

I reflected back on my childhood in elementary school. We would open our devotion in the classroom with the Pledge of Allegiance. I'd repeat it with emphatic expression only to impress my teacher. However, as I got older and understood the real meaning of what I was saying, the words "with liberty and justice for all" became personal. Was it justice for all? In actuality, justice was not applicable for every American citizen at all—only if your skin was white. The implications were clear to me, and the pledge could have just as well read, ". . . liberty and justice for all except for the Negro." It was difficult to fight beside my white comrades in trenches and foxholes, not knowing which ones harbored the most hatred or hostility. The challenge was more than I'd bargained.

CHAPTER 6

It was about four or five months into the country when I got promoted from PFC to Specialist, which was the rank of an E-4. According to my officers, I was fighting well enough to advance to that position. Although I was glad to receive a promotion, it came with more responsibility. I remembered when I was in junior high. I always bragged with my cousin about being a soldier one day. We discussed in detail what we desired to do. His dream was to drive a tank for the Marine Corps, and I wanted to operate a machine gun. When I was promoted to take Big Daddy's place as a machine gun operator, I thought about what my cousin and I had said. At that time, it was innocent child talk. I didn't know that wishes really do come true.

I sat at a table in a card game with Big Daddy, Brody and a couple of Hispanic soldiers who'd just arrived. I looked up into the face of a sergeant with two more newcomers.

"This is PFC Connelly Hunter and PFC Billy Daniels," the sergeant said.

Wouldn't you know, I looked up into the faces of two white guys, looking to be around nineteen or twenty years of age.

"Specialist Dula will be your squad leader," the sergeant went on to say. "And you are his ammo barriers."

My eyes rose in surprise. Just my luck to have two white men assigned to me, I thought. By the looks on their faces, they were just as surprised as I was to hear that they'd be my ammo barriers. They gazed down at me as if it were the first time they'd seen a black man.

"Pull up a chair," I said.

Within seconds, one of them made a shocking remark that made my jaw drop.

In a thick Southern accent, he said, "We don't mean no harm, but we're prejudice. We're not used to being around black people."

"But don't hold that against us," the other guy added precariously.

His deep accent matched his friend's. They made that statement so calmly and politely that one would've thought it was part of an award ceremony speech. The interesting part, they looked sincere. Though spoken in all honesty, it was amazing to me they didn't know how serious that statement meant to a black man.

Both men stood straight with their shoulders tucked back as if they thought the comment was necessary for any other future conversation with us. I wondered if they were members of the Klu Klux Klan.

My agitated look must have been obvious to my sergeant. He started fidgeting and got quickly to the rest of his speech.

"Sergeant Dula will fill you in on your duties and responsibilities," he said. Then he looked at both the newcomers. "I guess I'll leave you men to get acquainted." He turned and left.

Big Daddy took a deep breath and exhaled. He got up and leaned into Billy's face. His eyes were cold and daring. His jaws locked tightly. And then he spoke, quietly and calmly.

"Well, if you don't like chocolate milk, then you shouldn't have come in our kitchen," he said.

I looked into the white faces and thought to add. "I don't particularly like white milk, but it tastes pretty good with Oreo cookies."

I heard Brody chuckle. Across the room, a couple of black guys in the room overheard us and clapped, slowly in rhythm. Connelly and

Billy nervously traded glances. I was sure Big Daddy was going to give one of them a big punch with his fist. Surprisingly, he casually stuck a stick of chewing gum in the corner of his mouth while holding a shot glass in the other hand.

"Nothing like toasting over white milk and Oreo cookies," he said, as he held his glass up to them. He sat back down, rocked back in his chair and leaned against the wall. He wore a half grin when he said, "So, since we're all out here in this hell hole together, we might as well get along."

He took a swallow of his liquor and lifted his glass to Connelly and Billy.

"Now that we got that out of the way," he said. "Let's toast to white milk, black Oreos, and two crazy ass fools." There was utter silence. Big Daddy laughed and said, "For which we, by the way, don't hold that against them."

Everybody looked astonished. Suddenly, the other men in the room burst into peals of laughter. Before long, we all started laughing— all except Connelly and Billy who stood with flabbergasted looks. Big Daddy turned back to the card game.

I watched Connelly and Billy walk out of the club that night with their heads hung low. I don't think they quite understood how hard they rocked the boat with us black men. Racial issues were a sensible subject, ones for which to be reckoned.

I was growing weary about all of the wars—the fight for whatever we were there for in South Vietnam; for racial equality in America, and for the battle that was far more troublesome than any of the previously mentioned—my fight against loneliness and depression by being separated from Ava.

One evening at the NCO club, I decided to use my cordial manners my mother taught me and join Connelly and Billy at the bar.

"Where're you from?" I asked, turning to Connelly as he clutched a beer bottle.

"Nashville, Tennessee," he said.

Billy butted in. "My hometown is Birmingham. But I spent a lot of my time in Texas with my grandparents."

I couldn't believe it. Wouldn't it be my luck, I thought, to have two guys in my unit who weren't used to Negroes and who were from that neck of the woods—the heart of racial turmoil? It was as though I was being punished for some crime I didn't commit. I wondered how they felt and what their family was doing when the evening news reported the harsh treatment of blacks and civil rights protestors being dragged and beaten by policemen and white racists.

"What about you?" Connelly asked, breaking into my thoughts.

"Me . . . oh, well . . . I'm not from that part of the South," I said. "North Carolina's my home. Done a lot of travel further down, though."

"Doing what? Sightseeing?" he asked. His eyebrows rose. He seemed more interested in the conversation than Billy, who had excused himself to join some guys across the room.

"Nope," I said. "Got some friends down there."

"How long?" Connelly asked.

"How long . . . what?"

"How long your friends been there?" he responded.

"Don't know exactly, but it's been a long time," I replied. I pulled out my wallet to get a cigarette I'd squashed inside. Ava's picture appeared. Connelly glanced at the photo and back to me.

"Is that your girlfriend?" he asked.

"Not exactly," I said.

"What does that mean?" he asked.

"It's a long story," I said. "I don't plan to fall in love, again."

Like a cowboy who'd just entered a salon looking for a fight, Connelly took a gulp of his beer and wiped his mouth hard with the back of his hand. He burst into laughter.

"We'll see how long that lasts once you see the sexy Vietnamese woman the guys are talking about," he said.

"No, way," I said."I got a woman waiting when I get back home."

Connelly looked confused. "But I thought you said you'll never . . ."

"I know what I just said," I replied. I looked over at Connelly and noticed a minuscule portrait in the locket around his neck.

"That can't be your sister," I said.

"Hell, no that's my girlfriend!" he answered. "I don't carry my sister 'round my neck. Took getting drafted to get her off my back! I keep reminding her that she's not my mother."

I chuckled. "I know."

"You have sisters?" he asked.

"Yep," I said.

"How many?" he asked.

"Too many," I replied.

We laughed. The atmosphere between us warmed as the night went on. However, I wasn't letting my guard down. I didn't know what thoughts were going through his mind about me. And, I certainly wasn't trying to be his friend.

It wasn't long before we headed back to our hooch. No sooner than I had fallen asleep, I had a nightmare about Jerome and Ava. In the dream, they were cuddled on her sofa. Jerome looked like a Viet Cong soldier at first. I lunged for him, but then his face became clear. Before I could get my hands around his throat, Connelly shook me awake.

"Hey, man. Are you okay?" he asked.

"Yeah," I mumbled.

"You kept groaning . . . talking out of your head," he said.

"What did I say?" I asked.

He shrugged. "Couldn't make it out."

"I guess it's just jungle madness," I said. I turned over, but I couldn't get back to sleep that night.

In mid–August, orders were passed down for another mission. It would be the first time Connelly and Billy would be with me as my ammo barriers. I knew they were a little uncomfortable with my leadership as a black man and were carefully scrutinizing me. By the uncertainty on their faces, I figured they were wondering how well I was going to handle my first conflict as a machine gun operator. White officials deemed us unfit in earlier wars. We were suspected not smart enough to know how to fight. And even the few that were permitted to go into the military served in segregated units. The black soldiers were considered to be more suitable for cooking and cleaning than fighting in a war.

Soon, I thought, my skeptical ammo barriers would know if my skin color made the difference in how a war was fought.

My ability to see better in the dark was most beneficial at that point. We entered a place called An Loc. As soon as we landed into the LZ, an attack was upon us.

"Cover!" I yelled.

We were trapped in a fixed position to another one of the enemy's nefarious plots. I didn't notice him at first, but when I looked, Billy was standing in full view of the enemy.

"Move!" I ordered.

He didn't bulge. Shots were steadily coming. I let him have a hard kick with the tip of my boot right between his buttocks. He jerked back to himself, dropped to the ground and crawled to his position.

Connelly loaded a 50-round belt as I crawled out on the flank about three meters. I steadied my knees, rose to my feet and fired rapid bursts. Shortly thereafter, the firing ceased from enemy lines. We crouched low and waited for signs of another attack. Luckily, the bush got quiet.

"That was a remarkable move," Connelly said. His eyes were stretched wide with fear.

"Yeah," Billy echoed. "Remarkable."

I rested my head on the tip of my gun barrel and silently thanked God. Although I felt Billy and Connelly's accolades were genuine, they had no clue of the danger I was put in when Billy froze in the path of the Viet Cong.

"Hold the praises," I said. "You've got to think fast, or we'll all be killed. We've got a long time in this war."

After that mission, Connelly and Billy kept mentioning what I'd done in the field. I wasn't looking for glorious pats on the back. On the battlefield, I had only one thought in my head—survival.

I often wondered what my men were expecting from me. I knew they had a weird perception about a black man in authority over them, particularly one leading them in battle, but I wasn't sure what that perception was exactly. I didn't need to prove anything to anyone. I was confident I could take care of my responsibilities without any assistance from my two young suspicious, yet scared white assistants. We were in a war with many more surprises ahead.

I tried to stay in the NCO club a lot to keep my mind off Ava. But, nothing really helped. I saw a soldier with a letter. The envelope had a heart drawn on the flap. Ava's mail always had her lip prints on each corner of the pages. It hurt to hear love ballads. But every time I'd go to the NCO club, I'd drift over to the reel-to-reel and play a sad love song. I had kept things she'd sent—particularly a dollar bill where she'd scribbled more zeros as a reminder that I would be a millionaire one day from my baseball career. I kept a poem she'd torn out of a book and some pictures of us at the lake. I reminisced about our many walks on the beach and wondered if she was spending time there with Jerome. I worried that I'd never get over Ava.

One night at base, I took out the Bible my mother had sent me. I never read it much. Every time I went out on a mission, I'd tuck it in my jacket. It became a safe storage for Ava's pictures. I pulled one of her pictures and stared at it for a moment. She wasn't looking her best that day, having just gotten over the flu. Her eyes were puffy from a fever, she said. She wore no foundation and bags hung underneath her eyes. She never wanted me to take that picture, but regardless of her appearance, she was still pretty to me.

I put the photo back in the Bible and was about to close it when my eyes fell on a passage in the Book of Solomon. My eyes traveled down and stopped.

Behold, you are beautiful, my love, behold,
you are beautiful
Your eyes are doves behind the veil
Your hair is like a flock of goats, moving
down the slopes of Gilead.

I was stunned. I didn't know words like these were in the Bible, so I was compelled to read on.

Your lips are like a scarlet thread,
and your mouth is lovely . . .

I shut the book and meditated on the passage of scripture. Was it coincidental I'd read the words so pertinent to me and Ava from the ancient pages of the Holy Bible? Was that a sign not to worry, that

Ava would once more be mine? Not knowing how things were going to turn out with us, I silently prayed for strength to hold on. I wasn't sure if God heard me, but I thought it wouldn't hurt to try.

I joined several men in a card game and regretted it later. All the talk was about women. Some guy was parading a picture of his wife and children. Another one was sharing a picture of him and his girl on a beach. He was bragging about their week in the Virgin Islands. I wanted to say, "For once, lay off of it!"

I used to boast about Ava to everybody back home. Sadly, I was now a walking time bomb about to explode.

I left the men. No one saw my tears. I'm sure I wasn't the only man in the military that was dealing with depression and loneliness. But I thought I was the only soldier who'd let it get the best of him.

After a couple of days, we were sent to Ben Cat. My division, the Big Red One, was a very mobile unit and could be called out in a moment's notice to go wherever necessary. The heat was sweltering. As we traveled through the bush, I'd stopped to wipe sweat that poured from my forehead onto my eyelids. Brody caught up with me.

"You haven't lit one up yet? he asked.

"Nope," I said. "And, I don't plan to."

He chuckled. "As uptight as I've seen you, it'll make a whole lot of difference."

"I can make it without it," I said. "I have this far."

"You know, people tell lies about smoking a joint," he said. "People think it'll make them go crazy and all that shit. You just get calm, you know. Like when you killed that gook out there, you should've come over my way. You would've felt a whole lot better."

I wasn't buying his explanation. I rushed to catch up with our squad. We traveled through the jungle with machetes, cutting away the thick grass, vines, and bamboo stalks. It wasn't long before I had an appreciation for the things I'd taken for granted, especially good clean water. Sometimes, my throat was dry and scratchy from dehydration.

We had small breaks when the CO decided we needed them. They lasted about fifteen or twenty minutes. Then we had to proceed with our mission.

Aside from having to search and destroy the enemy, we had to look out for the jungle creatures that were just as deadly. We were invading their homes. Large insects clung to trees and flew in front of us. We crushed under our boots mounds of huge red fiery ants and some insects I couldn't identify. The mosquitoes were horrendous. I swatted one that left a sting on my hand that looked like three or four bumble bees struck at one time. I was fearful of mosquito bites, because malaria had already spread like wild fire across the country.

The jungle held an ominous, eerie feeling. I jumped at every creepy sound.

Big Daddy was about four men ahead of me. His tall stature made it easy to keep him in view. He was someone that I didn't want too far away from me, because I drew strength from him. Nothing seemed to unnerve him.

We finally arrived at our designated location. Connelly help set our flares and claymore mines. We went back to join the other men who were settling in our dugouts. An uneasy feeling loomed over me. I knew something was wrong. I told Connelly to cover me while I went back to check the mines we'd just set. I don't know what led me back, but when I got there, I found one of the mines Connelly had set. It was placed backwards, pointing to our position. Carefully, I turned it around facing the direction of the enemy. Satisfied I'd gotten the mines in the right position, I stood up and froze with shock as I gazed at the back of "Mr. Charlie" as we called the Viet Cong. He hadn't seen or felt my presence, but I could clearly see his full stature only a few yards in front of me. I was helpless, alone without a weapon. This is it, I thought. I'm a dead man. Where's my backup? I knew Big Daddy strobe light was mounted on his gun as he watched me, but I wondered why he didn't fire.

I was alone and had to move fast. Just as I decided to take the chance and tackle the soldier, a shot came from our position. The soldier dropped.

Heat rushed to the top of my head. In a few moments a host of Viet Cong would be upon us, I thought. I ran as fast as I could toward our fixed position. Before I'd reached my destination, just as I'd predicted gunfire blasted from enemy lines. Charlie was in the thick jungle about fifty yards from us. I heard Big Daddy's strong, demanding voice.

"Down!"

We fought back hard and radioed for help. Charlie was not letting up. We pushed the enemy farther into the village as we continued receiving heavy mortar fire. A few moments later, we heard our tanks from the 11th Calvary. When they arrived, we turned on the enemy and began what was called a night assault. It was a fierce fight. That night, we fought about thirty minutes before the enemy broke contact. Luckily, we didn't lose any men. Only a few suffered injuries.

We helped our wounded men onto the chopper. I loaded our gear and headed back with the others to base camp.

I thought about the narrow escape with the Viet Cong. Even if I'd grabbed him from behind, I didn't have a chance with an armed man. I was thankful I was alive, but I was no fool. I knew sooner or later my luck would run out.

CHAPTER 7

Some men asked me to go with them into the village club for drinks and a little fun. The unit had returned from the bush. I joined several tired, weary looking men and headed out.

The war was taking a toll on me, too. My body ached, the slightest thing was irritating, and it was hard to stay awake even in a room with boisterous men and women.

An upbeat song played on the jukebox. Two of the women grabbed Billy.

"Wanna dance, G.I.?" one of them asked.

Both of them started twisting their hips, seductively, and dancing around him. He danced off beat, pressing his body into one of them and laughing all the time. Connelly joined in and tried to keep up with the other feisty Vietnamese woman, but she shook her booty all around him. A raucous laughter filled the room from the men across the room.

Big Daddy sat beside me at the bar. He yelled at Connelly, "Hey, didn't somebody tell you backward ass white people that you can't dance?"

There was another burst of laughter from the crowd. By now, Billy and Connelly were getting a handle on this racial thing and laughed right along. Finally, Connelly had enough trying to keep up with his wild dancer and staggered off the floor. He walked over to me.

"You should try that, Ken," he said. "I haven't felt this damn good in a long time."

He slid on a stool beside me. There was a pungent smell of liquor on his breath.

Big Daddy took Connelly's woman by the arm. "Let me show you white boys how it's done," he said, calling to Connelly.

He pulled the short, flirtatious Vietnamese woman onto the floor and started swinging her around. He let go of her hand and did a two-step slide. She giggled and fell back in his arms. Everyone started applauding. Big Daddy knew he had all of the attention, so he clowned even more. When the song had played out, he came back to the bar and slapped Connelly on the back.

"That's all there is to it," he said with a chuckle. "Stick around and I'll teach you white boys some rhythm. Ain't that right, Carolina?"

I nodded.

Brody slid on the seat beside me. "What's on your brains?" he asked, as he grabbed a drink off the counter. I shrugged.

"Look, you need to get you one of these village broads over there," he said, pointing to the corner of the room where three women were standing. "That's what they're here for, pal. Loosen you up a bit. You're tighter than a bolt on a tire rim."

I didn't answer. I looked over at the women. No doubt about it. They were knock-outs and much to be desired. As if one of them read my mind, she turned and walked over to me. Big Daddy winked at me and walked off.

She was a knockout, to say the least, and much to be appreciated if a man was feeling his lowest. Her long black hair hung loosely over one side of her face, creating a sexy look. She had the most gorgeous, silky skin I'd ever seen on a woman. Her fragrance was soft and nice.

"GI, Cho Phi my name," she said.

She stood over me with a million-dollar smile. Brody nudged me.

"Go on," he said. "And, all you need to give her is Saigon tea." He chuckled and walked off.

I stared at her for a second. Then someone popped a coin in the jukebox, turning the tempo to a slow, mellow beat.

"Wanna dance?" she asked.

I took a deep swallow of my beer. She moved closer to me, forcing her breasts gently against my arm.

"GI troubled?" she asked. "I give you boom, boom."

I'd learn that meant she wanted to have sex with me. She removed the beer from my hand and set it on the table. My eyes raked her body and then back to her face.

Why not? It'd been a long time since I'd felt a woman's skin next to mine or even looked into one's eyes.

She took my hand and led me to the back of the club behind a curtain. A cot sat in the corner with a ruffled blue spread on top. She unbuttoned my shirt and removed it. She then slipped her small fingers through my T-shirt. Her fingers move slowly, sending warm chills through me. I watched her slip out of her blouse, displaying her red bra.

"I good for you," she said. "I number one for you". She leaned over and kissed my cheek, my neck and finally found my lips.

I relaxed and let her move on top of me. She tossed her jet black hair her to one side. The moment was magical, until without a hint it was coming, I had a flashback of Ava. I remembered the way I felt holding her the last night we were together. I wanted her in my arms. I didn't want to feel another woman's body next to mine. Cho Phi wasn't Ava.

Cho Phi pressed against me. Her tiny frame moved slowly as she made quick, faint groans. I kissed her lips, trying to push Ava's face from my mind. Cho Phi repeatedly whispered in my ear "I good to you, GI. You're my man."

I wanted to push her away. It's not what she needed. I couldn't be what she wanted me to be—her man. But I couldn't resist, either. I surrendered and closed my eyes.

About twenty minutes later, I reached for my shirt and pants at the edge of the cot. The room felt chilly. There wasn't enough warmth from Cho Phi's body that could cure my ache for Ava.

"I gotta go . . ." I groaned, pushing Cho Phi to the side.

"GI, what's wrong?" she asked, pulling the bedspread over around her nude flesh.

I had sex with the wrong woman. That's what is wrong—severely wrong, I thought. Ava was everything, in everything and everybody. I had been with one of the most beautiful Vietnamese woman in town. Yet, there was no relief from the ghost of Ava. Where could I run from this misery? When will I be all right?

"Stay long time with me," Cho Phi pleaded.

I didn't want to be rude, so I promised her I'd spend the night with her the next time I saw her. She smiled and nodded.

When I walked back to the bar, I saw Big Daddy out of the corner of my eye talking to a couple of men. I slipped out of the village club without him noticing me.

Billy found me outside and walked over. His smile had changed to solemnity. "I've been meaning to tell you how sorry I am for making that remark the day I first met you," he said.

"What was that?" I asked.

"'Bout not liking black people," he said.

I'd forgotten about that first day we were introduced. Frankly, I wished he had, too.

"A man's got a right to his own opinion," I said.

"Well, I really don't have an opinion about it," he said. "It's just how we were raised. My parents didn't take too kindly to blacks, and they taught us to do the same."

I was annoyed until I looked in his face and realized he was trying to give me an honest apology. I straightened up to hear him out.

He hung his head. "When I saw how you men didn't jump all over us the first day, and it didn't bother you guys that we had those views, it made us think hard about what we'd said."

Connelly walked over. He'd overheard the conversation.

"What Billy is trying to say is we got it all wrong," he said, looking wide-eyed.

"It was stupid of us," he said.

"I don't understand," I said. "My skin hasn't changed."

"All that talk was bullshit," Connelly said. "We're not like we said we were. Not liking blacks and all. We're grateful that you guys were cool with that dumb statement."

I chuckled underneath my breath.

"No, no . . . don't get it wrong," I said. "We weren't cool about it. We just decided it wasn't worth arguing. Nothing was cool about us."

Connelly and Billy looked at each other for a second. I think they were afraid of what I'd say next."No hard feelings here," I said, placing my hand over my heart.

"By the way," Billy said. "Thanks for saving my life."

"I don't need you to thank me for that," I said. "Isn't that what soldiers do for each other, right? It's our duty, our oath."

"Yeah, you're right," Connelly said. "We just wanted you to know that . . ."

"It's okay. We're cool," I said, smiling. "Besides, nobody can hold one to his own ignorance, right? Let's put it behind us and move on. What do you say?"

The men looked like I had handed them a million dollars. We walked back inside the club. Connelly signaled for the bartender. "Hey, over here," he said. "Bring us a couple of beers. We feel like celebrating."

I had to admit, I felt better about the two white Southerners after they offered their sincere apologies. We shared personal stories that night. I told them about my ancestral heritage, that my family was culturally diverse.

They listened attentively as I spoke about my great, great grandfather, Squire Dula, who was Irish. "

"He was married and had eleven children by his white wife and ten other children by his black mistress," I said. "It took a long time before I knew there was mixed blood in my family. The family got so big, extending to cousins, aunts, and uncles until he decided to buy a large portion of land that each of us could own. He named our community Dula Town, after his surname.

I mused at the look on their faces. It was a shocker to them, I could tell.

"Our family was known throughout the entire town," I went on to say. "Lots of us owned businesses. The name Dula could be found on a grocery store window, a street sign, and churches. There was even a hospital named after our family. And the famous song entitled 'Tom Dooley' was written about one of my cousins accused of killing his girlfriend. Of course, like us, many of the town people felt he was innocent."

When I finished, Connelly and Billy were quiet at first. Then Billy cleared his throat and swallowed hard.

"That's quite a story," he said.

"It's not just a story, it's a true life story," I said.

"Well, like we said, our parents pressed us into thinking blacks were bad," Connelly reiterated. "They told us that if we associate with colors that we'd be just like them, dumb and stupid."

"I had black friends, but they were forbidden to come to my house," Billy said. "I never could understand that. They had never done anything to my parents or me."

"We did as we were told and asked no questions," Connelly said.

"So, you can see why we feel like we do about whites, right? I said. "Imagine going into a restaurant and before you can order you're told, 'We don't serve colored people'."

Connelly and Billy were silent for awhile. Then, we changed the subject and spent the rest of the evening talking about the war and what we were going to do if we got back home.

I learned a valuable lesson that day—to save judgment before hearing the whole story of a person's life and his upbringing. Connelly and Billy were acting out what they were taught, that blacks were subordinate and the white race, superior. I was responding from what I saw and knew—injustice and ill treatment of the black race, defenseless under the laws of Jim Crow. Both promoted a system of cruelty that was created by people with power, greed, and hatred. None of which were our beliefs or doings. They were as much victims of racial bias as I was of racial injustice.

One evening at base, Billy saw the Bible on the side of my cot.

"Are you Baptist?" he asked.

I sighed. The one question I feared was asked. I didn't know what I believed. Personal interpretations of the Holy book always caused a great deal of controversy. I tried to stay away from discussions about religion and politics.

"No . . . not really," I said.

"My mom is religious," he said. "I never tried to get into that stuff . . . too many parts of it that I can't understand. She asked me to go to church with her before I left. I went, but I didn't really want to."

He paused, shrugging his shoulders.

"You know how it is," he went on to say. "You don't know what to believe sometimes."

I nodded. "Yeah, I know."

"You read that Bible a lot?" Billy asked.

I sighed heavily. He was forcing me into a conversation I didn't want to have. I obliged him and made light of the subject.

"My mother is Pentecostal," I said. "In her church, they tell you to press on until he comes. Comes upon you, that is. I tried that. I stayed on my knees at the altar for nearly an hour. I don't think God knew I was there. He never showed up."

Billy laughed. "That's a good one."

"I learned one verse from Sunday school when I was a child," I said.

Before I could say another word, we heard a thumping sound from a distance.

"Cover!" My voice was strong, but my insides were shaking like mad. Then, BOOM! A mortar round landed within yards of our hooch.

We dived to the floor where several other soldiers had taken cover. A few more rounds fell near us, followed by silence. Then I looked over at Connelly. Sweat beaded on his forehead. He looked at me with his eyes stretched in fear.

"What bible verse is that?" he asked.

I laughed and said, "Jesus wept."

The mail arrived the next day. I was the first in line as I waited anxiously to see if I'd hear from Howard. I got a letter from my mother, as I often did, but that was it. There was nothing from Howard—not even a postcard. I slumped down onto a nearby crate.

One soldier saw me. "You know how the mail piles up before it gets to us," he said. "If you didn't get what you are looking for in this stack, it'll probably be in the next."

It was true. There was no certain pattern for which mail arrived. It took several weeks for it to get to us and sometimes in the bush, we didn't get it all. I understood that, but it didn't help much.

Although I was disappointed that Howard had not written, it was good to hear from my mother. She talked about the church, the things my father had done around the house, and how much she missed me. Surprisingly, she never once mentioned Ava.

Along with her letter, my mother had sent me a huge package. The guys gathered around like kids to Santa Claus as I rummaged through the box. Whenever any one of us got gift packages, we'd all share. However, I cleverly hid my hot sauce, something I refused to share with anybody.

Billy sat down beside me, waiting anxiously.

"Hallelujah! It's gonna be a good day," he said. His mouth twisted as he gazed at the stack of goodies. "I knew the good Lord was looking down on me last night and heard my humble cry."

Inside the box were canned goods, cookies, toilet tissue, lotion, and a few comic books that my mother knew I liked. A couple of tubes of Chap Stick fell out and a bottle of hot sauce. No one, except a soldier, will ever know what a tube of Chap Stick or a pack of chewing gum means to him.

Billy talked about as much as our platoon sergeant. I was half listening to him as I dug in for the rest of my things. He sat back and thumbed through his mail.

"I got a letter from my girlfriend, Andrea," he said. He smiled, as he pulled out a portrait stuffed in a brown envelope. I took a peep at the tall, slim brunette, seemingly around seventeen or eighteen with a long pony tail thrown over one shoulder.

"She's graduating from UCLA in the top ten percentile of her class," Billy said. "She's only made one B in all four years."

I wasn't in the mood to hear about his girl. But, to be polite as I was taught, I forced a smile back and asked. "Do you think there's a future with her?"

"Maybe one day," he said. "She keeps asking, but I told her I can't think about it while I'm out here."

"Women like for you to make decisions at the strangest times, don't they?" I asked.

"Yeah, but I'm not going to lose hold of myself," he said. "Gotta keep a level head, you know."

He lit a cigarette and offered me one. I removed the white beauty from his hand and lit it.

"It amazes me how many bad habits you pick up when you come in," I said, inhaling deeply. "I've never smoked this much before."

"Me neither," he said and took in a deep draw of tobacco.

Although I didn't feel up to talking about his girlfriend, I was curious as to how he really felt toward her.

"Are you in love?" I asked. "With what's her name?"

"Andrea," he said. He shook his head."I don't know. I don't want to tell her that I want to marry her until I know if that's really what I want to do when I get back."

"Well, you better know for sure," I said. "If you turn your back, Jody just might be in your sack."

"Why do you say that?" he asked.

"Nothing," I said. "It's nothing. Don't worry. You probably have someone who's faithful. I'm sure she'd never do anything like cheat on you."

Billy gave me a curious stare.

"Did that happen to you?" he asked.

I didn't answer, but quickly added. "From that picture, your gal's a humdinger like what we saw on the streets of Saigon. You are one lucky man!"

Billy laughed, nodding. "I know what you mean," he said. "But it's hard to resist what's in the village, you know."

We started talking about the Vietnamese village girls. From the smiles on the faces of the men who came from the village, the women always left a wonderful ineffaceable mark on them. The average height of the women was about five feet. They had small proportionate frames and walked with a quick twist of the hips. Each one of the women had a distinct personality, but their mannerisms were quite the same. They were persistent, yet gentle in their approach. Most of them were soft spoken. You had to listen very closely when they spoke. When they smiled, their deep brown eyes held a sparkle that lit up an entire room. But still, no matter what they were, they weren't Ava.

CHAPTER 8

In the middle of July, we were on a mission in Lai Khê—a city toward the north. It wasn't my lucky day. Cutting through the thick foliage, I walked as point man ahead of the company. Without warning, I walked up on an anti-aircraft MG. I was facing the enemy square in the face. I think we surprised each other. My knees weakened and my hands started to shake, violently when I saw his gun pointed at me. Death was staring me right between my eyes.

When the Viet Cong attempted to fire, his gun jammed. For a second, I felt like I was out of my body. I couldn't move. Then, as if someone jerked me away, I turned and ran as fast as I could. I alerted my company that the enemy was upon us. No sooner than I'd gotten to the others, we received incoming rockets and RPG firings. I fell for cover and returned fire with my men.

I heard the enemy's voices coming from my left. A small bush moved and a couple of Viet Cong appeared. I signaled to my men and pointed in the enemy's direction. They fired all at one time, dropping the Cong to the ground. In only a few seconds into the fight, several of our men had fallen a few yards away from me. I heard our lieutenant called for support.

We fought for hours before the conflict ended. When the gunfight ceased, I crumbled to my knees and thanked God for another narrow escape from death. Our choppers sprayed the area as medics rushed to the wounded. I watched as our injured men got loaded on stretchers, not knowing whether they were dead or alive. I saw no movement from any of them. Not even a slight lift of the head. I fought the urge to cry. It was hard to lose a comrade. I don't think any of us ever got used to it.

When we returned to base, I sat down that night in an Indian-style position in my hooch and meditated on the fact that I'd escaped the gun barrel of a Viet Cong. It was another miracle I couldn't explain, and I shuddered when I thought about how close I came to dying.

I checked in the pocket of my jacket to see if Ava's picture was still there. It was tucked, securely. I pulled it out and held it in my hand for a few seconds. On the back, scribbled in her handwriting were these words:

"I love you with all my heart!"
Ava

I ran my finger over the words. Oh, God! I have to believe I'll make it back to her. I said, quietly to myself.

I spent that night thinking about home, wondering what my sisters and brothers were doing. And I longed for a good drink of that fresh, mountain spring water. It was fall back home and summer weather was changing. I imagined the leaves turning from green to yellow, orange and deep red, painting the forest and hilltops with autumn rich colors. Winter would be approaching soon after that and the town would get its share of heavy snow. I fell asleep with the image in my head of white covered mountains and silver trees.

By September, 1968, the war was getting worse with no victory in sight. We were on another mission. This time, our backs were to the swift, raging river called Phu Loi River.

"The only recourse is to swim over," our sergeant said.

Swim? I would surely die, I thought. I could swim a little, but not enough to cross that river. It looked treacherous.

"You men go on without me," I said. "I'll stay and cover you."

Aside from the fact I couldn't swim, my weapon weighed about twenty-three pounds. There was no way I could go over without drowning. By the look on Big Daddy's face, I could tell he knew I was afraid.

"I don't think any of us will make it over," he said. "It's a lot of water."

Our sergeant looked at Big Daddy and back to me. "Well, we'll just have to fight from here."

He turned to the others. "Okay, men. We're going to set up perimeters here," he said.

That was the day I saw the military's commitment to its slogan "No man left behind". It was the first time I realized how significantly bonded we were. I was accustomed to seeing our men pulling the dead and wounded from the bush, but I'd never known a company of soldiers to pause because one man couldn't cross water. We set up perimeters. Then about twenty minutes later, we caught fire from the enemy. Our backs were pinned to the river. I had gotten pretty good using my M-60.

The Viet Cong struggled trying to retreat as we pounded them continuously and violently. We knew there were innocent people in the village, but there was nothing we could do about it.

We kept moving inland toward the village, dodging bullets and firing back. Some of our men had fallen, and I rushed to help pull them out of the line of fire. I looked up and saw Big Daddy struggling through the line of fire as he carried a man on his shoulder like a shepherd with his lamb. He dropped the wounded soldier down beside me. His leg was bleeding, and there was a large cut on his right hand.

In a distance, I heard a woman groaning. "GI . . . help," she cried. I looked in her direction. Big Daddy saw me as I started toward her position.

"Don't you dare do it," he warned. "She may be your death ticket."

The woman's cries were agonizing. She moaned consistently, calling out for help. Her voice grew fainter and fainter until finally, there were no sounds at all.

"The enemy use women sometimes to beckon for us, and when we get to them, they blow our damn heads off," Big Daddy said.

It was hard for me not to reach out to the woman. Even though there was distress and much suffering among the people, the Vietnamese were friendly and very receptive when they saw us. Their hostility was not to Americans, but rather to the brutal regime of the Viet Cong. Looking in the faces of the innocent people, I fully understood a combat soldier's definition of war. It's hell on earth.

We pressed on until the enemy finally retreated.

After about an hour of fighting, our blessed gunships arrived, dropping fire rounds illuminating the area. I was about to follow my men when a burst of automatic gunfire erupted from our gunship. I leaped into thick foliage and fell headlong into a ditch, dodging friendly fire only a few yards from.

The sun rose and we were able to sweep the village. It was a gruesome sight. I had no idea we'd moved that far into the dwelling place of villagers. I stared at the long traces of blood where the enemy had dragged its own off the path to prevent us from knowing how many of them we'd killed. The one thing we knew by the amount of blood on the trail, we hit quite a few.

I walked soberly. It was the first time I'd looked into the faces of frightened villagers and on the destruction of their life's substances. All the livestock and animals were destroyed. The village people had been warned of the attack and were out of the way when the fight begun. But, as things settled, a few women and children came into view.

I watched as several of our men set fire to what remained of the village. I looked into the faces of the villagers whose homeland we destroyed, who undoubtedly had families they loved and a country they cared about, and I was flooded with guilt. I found it difficult to understand the war in which I fought. Innocent civilians and soldiers died daily—some with graves where no one mourned—while the governmental officials were shouting, "Let's overthrow communism, and let freedom ring." When the war is over and we leave the fields of Vietnam, I wondered if their freedom would ring. Would it ring for the men and women who harvested their grain for food through unsettling conditions and hard labor only to see it gathered in heaps of ruins? For boys and girls who watched their homes burn and play grounds destroyed? For the ones in hospitals who were left unattended while hundreds of wounded civilians and soldiers poured into overcrowded corridors? No soldier wants to kill, yet war provokes what he has been trained to do—sometimes, the unthinkable. As a result, the innocent civilians become the victims.

Later on that evening, I saw Big Daddy cleaning his rifle, and I sat down beside him.

"I can't take this," I choked. "These people have nothing left. The children have no homes."

"You ain't seen nothing yet," Big Daddy said, as he chewed on a paper straw. A chuckle rumbled in his throat. "Nah . . . nothing yet. In a few weeks, we'll fight in the Triangle. After that, I doubt you'll be sympathetic."

He put his rifle down and looked into my face. "One thing you'll learn out here," he said. "Tomorrow may never be yours. One soldier died out there today. He was only fourteen days from catching that Freedom Bird."

He picked his rifled back up and starting wiping it hard. "So, you see," he said. "You have to make a decision and it's simple. Live in the moment, and try to stay alive." He hunched me in the side. "Now let's go to the club, get some young babes and forget about what just happened out there."

I walked behind him to the NCO club with a lot on my mind. Every single day, men were dying on the hot foreign soil, and I grew more and more disheartened. We had suffered loss of men before, but this was the first time I'd experienced the lost of a comrade who was only two weeks from going back to America. There was no way of knowing how long the war was going to last. From the looks of it, we were in for a very long time.

Inside the club, the atmosphere was different this time. Conversation was at a minimal while the jukebox played a song "Bring the Boys Home" by Freda Payne. We kept telling the soldier at the jukebox to play it again. Although it was a sad song, it was as though we needed to hear it.

Fathers are bleeding, lovers are all alone
Mothers are praying, send our sons back home
You marched them away on ships and planes
To a senseless war, facing death in vain
Bring the boys home
Bring them back alive
Turn the ships around
Lay your weapons down
Can't you see 'em march across the sky

All the soldiers that have died
Trying to get home
Cease all fire on the battlefield
Enough men have already been wounded and killed
Bring the boys home
What they doing over there, when we need them over here?

I'd never seen the artist in concert, and some of the men like me had never heard of her before. But we acted as if she was our friend. One black brother shouted, "Tell the truth, sista!" The lyrics of her song made me feel like she really cared about the war and how we were faring. We were on the battlefield for weeks at a time. The loneliness was almost unbearable. It helped to know that a stranger, miles away who didn't know our names, understood us and could speak to our hearts even if it was only through a jukebox or reel-to-reel record player. I couldn't get the lyrics out of my head that night.

I saw Brody over in the corner of the room. He puffed lazily on a joint. His eyelids were about to close. And, then he saw me and gave a cocked smile.

"I'm telling you," he said, in a low voice. "You need to chill with me."

I shook my head and went to a corner of the room and crashed. That was the norm when I returned to base. I didn't do much more than think about Ava and sulk. She was on my mind more than the war, itself.

Before the week was gone, we bailed out on another mission. For the next six weeks, we would stop at Loi Khe. Our CO told us the 11th Armored Calvary Division was waiting for our arrival. They'd been operating in the area for several days.

When we entered the village, Big Daddy warned. "The enemy is good at making hand-made bombs and disguising them. Be suspicious even of the small children. Shortly after he spoke, we were put to the test. I encountered a young boy, around ten years old, walking up to me with something that looked like a rocket in his hand.

"Down . . . put it down!" I said. The young boy gave me a surprised and fearful look, and then he slowly laid the item down on the ground.

"Back . . . back!" I motioned with my hand.

The boy stepped back while one of our men examined the object. He discovered that it was a dead round, nothing at all harmful. I found out that the only thing the child wanted was to give me something in exchange for candy. I hugged the little fellow in relief, took in a deep breath and turned to Billy.

"That was too close for comfort!" I said.

"Hell, I almost pissed in my pants," Billy said.

"That little dude didn't know how close he came to getting shot," I replied.

We stayed in the village, searching for the enemy. Afterwards, we moved to another location.

As weeks passed by, we were losing men at base camp and in the field. The malaria problem had worsened. As the dreadful disease claimed soldiers every day, a couple of guys at base I'd grown close to had gotten very sick. Countless men were hospitalized and quarantined. Fortunately, as many times I'd gotten bitten by mosquitoes, the horrible disease never got me.

Leaving several sick men behind, we moved into other battlegrounds. We rushed through rapidly, hunting the enemy. Nearly two hours were spent in search of the Viet Cong.

It wasn't long before our luck ran out. As soon as we started making our way back to our perimeter,a Viet Cong sniper fired from a bunker, pinning us down. Suddenly, one of our men, who we called

"Lyles," stood up and said, "Damn these gooks! I'm gonna kill that son of a bitch!"

He leaped forward and fired hard. There's nothing like a combat soldier, especially a black man, who's had enough of the enemy. Lyles roared like a lion as he made a mad dash in open view. He then moved towards the bunker and shot the sniper. We knew Lyles had gotten the right one, because the firing ceased. Aside from observing Big Daddy who'd fought through enemy fire with a soldier across his shoulder, Lyles' action was as close to boldness I'd seen since I'd been in the war.

He walked back to us and said.

"Now that's what I'm talking 'bout!" he said. He was a light complexion black man whose cheeks were fiery red, and his eyes looked wild and crazy. I stared at the wide-eyed soldier in amazement. The other guys looked as stunned as I did at what he'd done. No one said a word. We crouched down and waited until it was safe to move on.

That evening, we ate and started with our jokes about who smelled the worse. We'd been weeks in the jungle without a shower, and our body odor was getting the best of us. A good joke made things better, because every moment was full of tension and fear.

A lot of buffalo meat had been prepared and packed by our cook at base camp. The food had been dropped to us earlier that day. The buffalo tasted like beef. I made another discovery about myself as I chewed on the meat that was tough as a rubber band. I realized I had stopped complaining. While in the bush, food of any kind is good.

That day we got an unexpected attack. A huge buffalo started toward one of the black brothers.

"What the hell!" I heard him say.

His eyes bulged as he pulled his M-16 and brought the wild ox to its knees. Unfortunately, the soldier who shot the buffalo was written up for violating the military code of conduct. I didn't blame him for shooting the beast. No one could take a hit from a buffalo unless he was made of steel. Coincidently, each time one of the huge animals would attack, it would always charge after a black soldier. We joked about that for a long time.

Word had gotten back to base that one of our companies burned the villages—an act forbidden in combat. We'd been given mandatory orders not to endanger the populated areas of civilians, even though any one of the homes could have been serving as a cover for the Viet Cong. Our captain flew over and saw the blazing fire. For punishment, our weeks of combat in enemy territory were extended to two more weeks. We all wanted to get our hands on the one who blew the whistle.

The wet trenches that held the smell of sewage were our only places of rest when there was no activity from the enemy. Settling into a spot in my poncho, I fished for my bandana and pulled out one of Ava's photos—the one I'd taken with her posing in her bikini bathing suit. I stared at her silky legs and recalled that late afternoon on a hot summer day in July.

We were going to the beach that day. When I arrived at her apartment, she was working on her scrap book. A stack of pictures was on the coffee table. I sat down beside her and started kissing her. My hot breath traveled on her neck and shoulders. I kissed her forehead and moved down her cheeks until I found her lips.

"Ken, you are breaking my concentration," she had said, giggling.

"You make me hungry for your love," I said, through pecks of tender kisses. Suddenly, I got this brilliant idea.

"Let me take a picture of you with no clothes on," I whispered in her ear.

"Ken!" she said. "Why do you want to do that?" she had asked, her eyes stretched wide. "Are you crazy?"

"Look," I said. "Nobody's gonna see it but me. I promise."

She giggled as she brushed her hair from off her forehead.

"I brought my camera," I said. "It's in the car."

"You planned this?"

"No," I said, urgently. "I thought we'd take some pictures at the beach today." I stumbled with my words. "So I stuck my Polaroid in my glove compartment."

Ava gazed into my face. Then she smiled, turned slowly and started toward the hall. It was exciting thinking about her undressing for me. We had made love in the backseat of my old Ford, but it was always at night. I'd never seen her from top to bottom, nude in front of me. I never thought she'd comply when I asked her, and I was completely shocked when she said, "Wait here until I call for you."

She had vanished through her bedroom door. I dashed out to my car, swung open the passenger's side and grabbed my camera from the glove compartment. Scraps of paper and pens spilled out onto the floor board.

I ran back inside. Once inside, I paced the floor as I waited with baited breath for her to call me. After a few minutes, I heard a soft beckoning.

"Kenneth, you can come now," she said.

Drunk with anticipation, I had headed down the hall, until I reached her door.

"Are you sure you're ready?" I had asked. The question wasn't for her but rather for me. I had to take a few moments to steady my hands.

"Yes," she said.

When I opened her bedroom door, my mouth dropped. She was breathtaking and beyond words of expression.

I fumbled with the camera as I tried to get the lenses focused at the right angle and distance. She wasn't nude, but the suit showed every inch of her perfectly proportionate, magnificent figure. I looked at her tiny waist, then to her full breasts protruding through the top of her navy blue bathing suit, displaying a huge peak of cleavage. She had positioned herself, posing like a trained model with one hand propped on her hip and the other over her thigh.

I guided the camera lenses up and down her body, studying every inch of her like a scientist with a microscope. Finally, I aimed and snapped a picture. She looked as if she wanted to please me, so she twisted to the side, giving me another pose. I snapped. Slowly, she stood up and gave me a seductive pose leaning against her dresser. I snapped a few more shots. Seconds later, simultaneously as if we both had rehearsed, her hand dropped to her side as I lowered my camera onto the foot of the bed.

I walked over and pulled her down onto the soft mattress. Her warm lips met mine and lingered. I felt a warm, inexplicable thrilling sensation traveling through me like rippling waves of water flowing from a brook. We'd kissed many times before, but this time it was different. I felt as if heaven was upon us that day.

I pulled away and placed my cheek next to hers. We both were silent. Did she feel that heavenly kiss? She must have. It wasn't magical, nor was there anything mystical about it. To say that would make us seem like two young teens who were infatuated. It was far passed the butterflies of puppy love. It was as though the Almighty, himself, had stepped into our intimate moment and sprinkled miracle love dust on top of our heads.

Ava had sat up, slowly.

"What was that?" she asked.

I wasn't imagining it. We both felt the same thing.

"You felt it, too?" I asked as I stared into her face.

She nodded. I pulled her back into my arms and held her tight. That feeling was far beyond words; far beyond human capacity of reasoning or human intellect; far beyond limits—beyond the universe.

"I have to get dressed," she said, moving slightly underneath me as she tried to get up.

I didn't want to let her go. I stroked her cheeks and caressed her shoulders. She groaned to my touch, and then suddenly she pushed up. Reluctantly, I released her from my embrace. She moved slowly across the hall to the bathroom. I was immobile, weak from the kiss that pulled me as it buried her love inside of me.

Billy dropped down beside me. I tucked the picture back in my bandana and placed it inside my jacket. I tried to keep my promise to Ava that only my eyes would see it. Billy rested his rifle beside me and unloaded his gear. "Two more weeks, man!" he said. "I'd like to know who screwed us up."

"Me, too," I replied.

My troubled thoughts returned. The longer our mission, the longer we'd stay in harm's way.

CHAPTER 9

We'd been four weeks in the bush without getting any letters. I was certain it would be my lucky day to hear from Howard.

I was always the first to get to drop site, but this time the men played a trick on me. When the mail arrived, three of them hid my mail from me. Big Daddy was one of them.

"You're losing your popularity," he said. "Nothing came for you today."

"His luck's finally run out," another soldier added. "He thought he was the only one who could get five and six letters at one time."

"Super Star, better known as Little Star," another soldier said.

They all burst into laughter.

I ignored the jokes. I noticed Big Daddy with one hand tucked behind his back.

"Man, stop playing with me," I said. "Where's my mail?"

The men roared with laughter.

"Com'on, man," I said. "Give it to me."

"How much you willing to pay me?" Big Daddy asked with a chuckle. When he saw I'd raise my hand to give him a blow with my fist, he pulled the stack out.

"Hold it!" he said, laughing. "Here it is. I don't want to lose my right jaw over it."

I got my stack of mail and thumbed through the bundle. There were two letters from my mother, one from a cousin, and one from a high school friend, but there was no sign of a letter from Howard.

I wasn't the only one that day who was distraught. A couple of the men in my outfit had received unfortunate heartbreaking news from home. They tried not to show their anguish. One guy, a Latino, dropped to the ground. His head swung from side to side as he wiped his eyes. I sat beside him.

"Bad news, I suppose," I said.

He nodded. I didn't say anything for awhile. Finally, he volunteered the information.

"She's calling our relationship quits," he said. "It's strange how you think you know somebody. I thought we had something, you know. I guess my hopes were up too high."

I nodded. We combat soldiers found it easier to fight the enemy than to deal with personal, sensitive issues of infidelity. Most of the time, if a man got such a report, he'd try to hide his hurt and laugh it off, but no matter how big the laughter or wide the smile, he couldn't hide the pain in his eyes. We didn't want to hear bad news of any kind—relatives dying, someone losing a job, or sickness in the family. It was enough trying to survive the war— dodging bullets, mortar rounds and unexpected ambushes. Through it all, though, we did our best to help each other in difficult times. The combat field was the best place in the world for bonding. We could count on the support from each other when dealing with harsh reality.

The guy balled up his letter and hung his head. I patted him on the shoulders. I had no words to say that would ease his pain. No ointment, no sedative, not even pain pills. It had been several months now since I last saw Ava. Watching him made it feel like the incident with her had just happened to me.

Finally, our extended punishment weeks were over. We moved to our third base camp, Quan Loi——the Red Mud city. I'm not sure how it got its name, but I didn't see a city of mud. The region was a tangled mass of untamed forest with rice patties all around. There was no sign of habitation anywhere other than our camp.

Despite the uncultivated land, the jungle was lovely with its perennial plants and foliage.

Sleep deprivation made me paranoid and edgy. I stopped caring about anything, good or bad. That kind of thinking was nearly fatal for me on the battlefield that day. Big Daddy and Billy helped me set up our perimeters as we dug in for the night. The jungle was quiet. An uneasy feeling crept over me. I had become aware of danger by the way my insides jumped when the enemy was near. I warned the other men of what I'd suspected. My instincts proved right, again. No sooner had we settled down, a blast of gunfire came from the thick trees. We hit the ground for cover.

The sounds coming from the AK-47 rifles were like the crackling sound of wood burning in a fireplace. The red tracer coming was scary and deadly.

Then, out of nowhere, boldness rose inside of me like an exploding volcano. I felt an incredible surge of strength. I jumped in the clearing and became an easy target for the enemy. I started firing my machine gun. Big Daddy grabbed my arm and jerked me down by the collar.

"Get your black ass down," he yelled. 'What in the hell are you doing? You're gonna get your ass killed like that!"

I could feel bullets zooming close to my head. For a moment, I didn't know what had happened to me or why I got that strange notion to do that. I wanted to leap forward and fight. It was then I understood why Lyles felt the urge to take on the enemy by himself. I suppose fatigue and depression had gotten to us, both.

I dropped down and took cover, thankful to Big Daddy for bringing me back to reality.

"What in the hell were you thinking?" Big Daddy asked. A deep frown was buried in his forehead.

"There's something about fighting at night that make me feel invisible", I said.

"Hell, naugh!" Big Daddy, said. "It's that damn liquor that got your brains fried."

Another day passed. I felt my strength fading. The stifling heat from the sun drained a lot of our energy. There were times when we had to walk five to ten miles in the bush without rest.

Along with the intense heat, we had to deal with the threat of danger posed by poisonous vines and humongous plants. When there was no toilet tissue and we had to go, we used whatever we could get our hands on. Very often, we would break off a leaf and use it as a tissue. There's nothing worse than an itch between the buttocks that far from base camp.

Things were quiet. For the next two days, we didn't encounter the enemy. The men told jokes and laughed to kill the morbid atmosphere.

One night a soldier got a surprise from a jungle creature. We were in our foxhole. One of my squad men was on a machine gun when I heard crawling sounds in the hole. I signaled to him to be still. We knew any time we set up an ambush that we had to be extremely careful not to make any noise. However, this particular sound was not from the enemy. I suspected it was a reptile or something close to it because of its movement. I told him as calmly as I could, "I think that's a snake I hear."

"Oh, shit!" he said. "What the hell . . ." He jumped up and starting brushes his arms and legs.

"Stay down," I said.

"The hell I will!" he said.

Before I could say anything more, he started running through the jungle. I could hear bamboo sticks breaking under his feet. After a few seconds, I saw him coming back.

"Why did you run, fool?" I asked. "You could've been killed."

He looked at me while still trying to catch his breath. "I almost shit in my pants!" he said. "I'd rather die from a bullet than by a damn snake any time!"

I buried my face in the cuff of my jacket to smother my laughter. It wasn't my intention to make light of the situation, but I couldn't help it. And, it felt good to laugh. It'd been a long time since I'd found anything funny.

We settled back down. Routinely, we had two hours on and two hours off for watch duty. After my watch, I was desperate for sleep. It was impossible, however, to close my eyes with ease. Snakes and stinging insects were easily right at our nose. And to make matters worse, I had terrible back spasms to go along with my insomnia.

Finally, having spent the extra two weeks in the field for punishment burning the village, our CO notified us that our mission was over. The thought of getting fresh water, a hot meal, and a bath was music to my ears. I'd never thought I'd be excited about returning to camp to a hooch with a dusty cot, a man-made shower stall, and a hole in the ground for a restroom.

Downtime was never long, so we took full advantage of it when we got it. The next day, we went straight to the small village club where the women were waiting for us GI's. Several women pranced around seductively with drinks on trays.

Across the room, concealed behind heavy curtains that dropped to the floor from thick ropes, were a couple of massage parlors. Curiously, I plowed through the crowd and headed to one of the rooms in the back. I pulled back the curtain and looked across the room to a table, padded with blankets, where Brody was pleasantly weak under the long strokes of a Vietnamese woman. The women had parlors all over the village. From what I'd heard, they were very good at what they did. Brody raised his head. His eyes drooped and a faint smile appeared.

"Carolina, this is one helluva ride," he said.

Before I could respond, a young girl pulled me over and started taking my shirt off. She motioned for me to get on the table. I followed her instructions and stretched out on the warm padded surface.

Her hands ran down my spine, gently . . . smoothly. I could feel my tight muscles giving way in my back and shoulders.

The young girl bent over, pressing her palms along the side of my lower back, then to the center and back out, again. I caught a wimp of a sweet scent from her long, silky hair that fell on my cheeks as she leaned into me.

It was the little things like massages that took my mind to Ava. Most often, she'd get in the mood to give me a good massage when we were on the beach. I imagined the warm summer breeze on my face, the sounds of sea gulls chirping overhead, and the touch of her soft, gentle hands on my flesh.

I imagined Ava's magical fingers moving firmly yet gently and rhythmically up and down my back. I missed her more than ever. Everything reminded me of her—the massages, the full moon on clear nights, and a familiar song from the jukebox that we both liked.

"I make you feel better?" the young girl asked.

"Yes . . . yes, indeed," I moaned.

After about an hour, the massage was over and the young girl waited for her pay. I slapped a few bills in her hand. She looked satisfied and led me to the door.

The jukebox was playing new releases of sounds from America—home sweet home. Brody and Big Daddy were at the bar.

"Well, Carolina," Big Daddy said. "My time is short".

"I know," I said, as I slid on a stool beside him. "It won't be the same without you."

"You men will be all right when I leave," he said. "Once you get them damn women off your brains!"

All of a sudden, out of the clear blue, one of the men started singing the lyrics to our boot camp song, "Jody's got your gal and gone".

That wasn't a good idea for that guy to do that. Instantly, I envisioned Ava with Jerome. Heat rippled through me. Wrong time, wrong song. Before I knew it, I was in his face.

"Shut the hell up!" I said.

The soldier was taken off guard.

"I'm sorry, man," he said with a surprised look. "I didn't mean to upset you." He staggered off.

I settled back down beside Big Daddy and gulped down a glass of beer. Big Daddy had a smile on his face.

"You need to yell a lot more," he said. "It takes those wrinkles out of your forehead."

"See, that's what I've been trying to tell him," Brody said. "He needs to loosen up. And I got just what he needs."

"You keep that shit to yourself," Big Daddy said.

He stuck his cigar in the corner of his lips and lit it.

He then took his Budweiser and held the bottle to my face.

"They lied to us, Ken," he said. He drew a line with his finger under "weiser".

"The name's misleading," he said. "It don't make you wiser, just makes you feel like you got some sense. You're still a dumb ass."

Big Daddy burst into laughter. Brody slapped him on the back.

"We all dumb asses," Brody roared in laughter. Several men overheard and joined them.

"I'll be leaving you girls in two months," Big Daddy shouted to the men. "Keep the faith and them sad songs off the jukebox." He held up a beer for a toast.

One highly intoxicated soldier, with a steep southern accent, sang loudly and out of tune, "Country road take me home, to the place where I belong. . ."Several men joined in. "West Virginia, mountain momma, take me home country road."

We all toasted to Big Daddy. I was happy for him, but I knew it wasn't going to be easy to see him leave. There was never a dull moment with him. And, watching him in combat was like watching the Incredible Hulk.

He clowned around quite a bit that night. I guess he was feeling pretty good about getting near the end. I'd been counting the months I had left. Each day seemed to grow longer, especially on the battlefield.

One of the men leaned across me and said to Big Daddy. "You know, I'm on that same ticket. *If* we make it out of here and get on the good old USA soil, I'm not gonna just kiss it. I'm gonna bury my head in the ground."

Even though the soldier made a joke out of it, I could see the uncertainty on his face when he made that statement. We all knew that it was a great possibility we could get to the very day of leaving the country, and the unexpected could happen.

Fresh turtles continued to come in to replace those who were fortunate enough to go home. New replacements got that name because it took them so long to get to us.

Sadly, we said our goodbyes to some guys who had served their time and were on their way home. As I watched them board the chopper, a part of me left with them. Once you spend days and hours together in the rice patties, trenches and wet foxholes, it never got easy saying farewell.

One day while I had some downtime at camp, there was a loud thump outside my hooch. I heard a soldier yell, "Mail call."

My heart raced. I leaped forward, brushing past a couple of men as I rushed toward the mail drop.

I waited, holding my breath for a letter from Howard. Every time I stood in line, my chest tightened and a knot came in my stomach. My hopes spun high and anticipation increased.

That day, it looked like three men in front of me had gotten letters from their sweethearts. I could tell by the huge smile on their faces. They went off to the side to read. After the last name was called, I stood alone with nothing in my hand—not even a letter from my mother this time.

I felt like the kid at Christmas who'd waited for Santa Claus to send him a new bike only to discover that Santa forgot. So I returned to my old familiar toy—the jukebox with its sad songs.

At times, I didn't know whether it was my stubbornness or my foolishness that caused me to cling on to the hope that Ava and I would be together again. It was hard to let go. I tried to hate her, but I couldn't. I tried to forget her and relax with the village women, but I couldn't even do that. I kept on waiting for mail from Howard no matter how many times I got disappointed.

It was impossible not to show my anguish, and I hated it when one of the men would notice how dreadful I looked after stepping out of the mail line.

Billy walked up and put his hand on my shoulder.

"It gets better," he said.

He and Connelly hung around me all the time now. We never talked about racial prejudice anymore after the day they apologized.

I didn't comment. Billy's sympathy, though genuine, didn't bring any comfort at all. He wasn't walking in my shoes. He wasn't crying inside, revamping the memories of the woman he loved and what they'd shared. He wasn't stabbed with nightmares or images of his woman and another man—images that left him blinded with madness.

I dragged myself back to my hooch and sat on my cot. A warm breeze came through the entrance. One of the men in camp had said to me one day, "If you write your feelings on paper it makes you feel better." He'd written in his journal about his feelings when his mother died. "It helped a lot," he had said. So, I decided to give it a try.

I found a pad, sat back and started to write about my feelings concerning me and Ava. Unfortunately, I couldn't get past the first two lines I scribbled in pencil. "I love her. She hurt me. I can't go on without her."

I balled up the piece of paper and tossed it. In a weird kind of way, I wondered if I truly wanted to be healed. I wondered if I enjoyed wallowing in my self-pity and used it as an excuse to be alone. By now, I'd become accustomed to depression and grief. They were my companions, hanging around like an old dog to his master.

I wondered if Ava thought about me at all. I imagined her standing at the door, peering through the screen. I closed my eyes and saw her face glowing under the front porch lantern. I thought about the last night we were together. She had opened the door and reached for my hand, locking her fingers into mine. I could hear her funny giggle that made me smile every time she laughed.

The last night we were together before I left for basic training, she never stopped talking about what we were going to do when I got out of the army. It was inconceivable to me that her desire for me was all pretence.

Before I fell asleep, I read an old letter from her, the only one I kept and couldn't destroy. I got to the end and stared a few seconds at her closing. "I will be right here when you return" it read. I folded the aged sheet of paper and stuffed it back under my cot.

My mind wouldn't shut down that night. I remembered her sitting in the bleachers at my ball game with her thighs exposed—an incredible view from the field that almost caused me to strike out. Now that I look back, I I'm sure she was deliberately flirting with me. She had her eyes on me for a long time, and I didn't have a clue. She hit the bull's eye of my heart with her cupid bow. I could clearly see her seductive gestures—the toss of her bangs from her forehead, the slight twist of her hips when she knew I was watching. I was a sucker for her, with no one to blame but myself. She had me, all of me. I was barely surviving in both battles—in the jungles of Vietnam, and inside my head, the images of her. Somewhere in between, I had to find myself. For the life of me, I didn't know how or if I'd ever do it.

CHAPTER 10

The sun was blazing down on us early that morning when we flew out of our base camp in Quan Loi and crossed into hostile territory. The TET offensive was about to increase all over Vietnam. Our duties were to set up an ambush at the location designated. Very often my mother's words came to me, "You will be wounded . . ." I got a bad feeling every time I thought about what she'd said. No doubt, I had been warned.

Several days passed, and there was no enemy activity. It was extremely hot and we all smelled like cow manure. As usual, we dipped water from the holes, splashed it on our faces and necks to cool us. Once we gathered our containers full of water from a mud hole, we'd drop a purification tablet in it, turn it up and drink. Mechanically, I forced the water down like all the other times. To say the least, I grew quite appreciative for the good old USA.

When night fell, we moved on through the bush. I looked over at Connelly. He'd been quiet for a long time.

"How are you doing?" I asked.

"Not good," he said.

I paused for a second and listened. Some may call it a sixth sense, but as strange as it may seem, I could sometimes feel when the enemy was near. A creepy sensation would come over me.

We traveled about a click, searching with our back and front eyes. Then, without warning, all hell broke loose. We heard the whistling sound for which we were so accustomed. Our sergeant's yell was petrifying. "Take cover, now!" I saw two of our men fall as rapid fire blasted our positions.

Like a python, the TET offensive was showing its ugly head, striking unexpectedly once more. This time, we'd walked into an ambush. I couldn't remember any Bible scriptures my mother used to repeat to me, but I needed to say something quickly. Under my breath, I whispered, "Forgive us our trespasses." That's all I could remember of the Lord's Prayer. I fired my weapon as hard as I could.

The enemy seemed to be well-equipped and heavily supplied with AK-47 rifles, mortars, RPGs, and rocket launchers. We were encountering a stubborn and determined enemy that showed no signs of retreating. They were fierce, unrelenting.

After about an hour and a half, the firing stopped. We stayed in our location until daybreak. Then around midday, we went out on a reconnaissance mission. It wasn't long before we spotted a regiment of hardcore North Vietnam regulars, dressed in uniform, well-equipped and moving toward Saigon. I estimated a regiment of over three hundred men moving in a rush.

Our lieutenant was anxious and wanted to engage the enemy.

"Listen up," he said, looking at us. "We're going to fire on them."

We all were stunned. I took my position as squad leader. I wasn't sure how my statement was going to settle with him, but I knew having just arrived in the country, he was raw.

"Sir, if you fire on what I'm looking at, they will overrun us before God can get the news," I said. "We're outnumbered about twenty-six to one."

My statement took him aback. I could tell by the frown and hard look he gave me, he didn't care to take instructions from me, a black man. And, I took a bold move, being that he ranked over me. But at the moment, I didn't care. Besides, we all agreed. No one was ready to self-destruct.

I urged him, "I'm asking you to carry out the order we were given, to report back to base and leave the B52 bombers to destroy the area."

He nodded, and I took a deep breath. I was grateful that he listened to me. I didn't mind letting him know his desire to attack was profoundly ridiculous. The choices made on the battlefield determined whether a soldier lives or dies. I wasn't about to find out who was a hero through trial and error.

The regiment moved on.

While we were in the field, we'd gotten the report that the enemy aggression had magnified. Hospitals were filling up all over the country because of the intense fighting in the TET offensive. The mission was living up to its name—The Hobo Woods—war in the belly of a whale.

We stayed in the field about two weeks with no word when we'd leave. The fight was taking its toll on me. And from the looks of fatigue on the other men, it was getting the best of them, too. We were hungry and thirsty and most of us were completely worn out. Nonetheless, I knew we had to hold out. A tired body can cost a life.

I took out Ava's photo and looked at it for a moment. I longed to see her face, again. Howard would write, I was certain of it. I mustn't give up!

After another week, we received word that our mission was complete. The idea of returning to base changed the atmosphere entirely. We couldn't gather our gear fast enough. I think we all looked forward to getting back to the NCO club for drinks. Most of the men talked about going into the village for some wonderful massages. That didn't sound bad to me, either.

When we arrived at base, I headed to the club and passed a group of jubilant brothers shooting a ball through a hole in a bucket. Someone had made a basketball hoop and attached it to a pole he'd dug into the soil. When I walked inside the club, I saw our lieutenant at a table with three other men. He got up slowly and walked over to me.

"Thanks for the warning," he said. "My mind wasn't in the right place out there for what I was feeling."

His eyes dropped and his voice cracked when he said, "I lost my best friend in this war. The only friend I had." His eyes held anger and pain. He then turned and walked off. It made sense to me now. He wanted revenge.

My idea of winding down was listening to music. I dropped a coin in the jukebox and crawled into a chair against the wall. Then I overheard Brody and some men talking about the Iron Triangle.

"Your unit is scheduled for the Triangle in a few days," I heard Brody say. "I got damn lucky, man. I'm not on that mission."

"By what I hear, none of us may come out alive," another soldier answered.

The conversation was morbid. I tried to shut their voices out by humming to a country western song that was playing on the jukebox.

A few minutes later, Connelly and Billy walked in. I didn't think they saw me at first, and I was hoping they wouldn't. But, they did and sauntered over. Connelly pulled out a cigarette and offered one to me.

"We don't think we're going to make it out there," Connelly said, as he lit his tobacco and mine.

"But you will, Carolina," Billy said.

I looked at them both, curious as to why they'd think I would make it and they wouldn't.

"That's crazy talk," I said. "You guys are my ammo barriers. But, more than that, you feel like my flesh and bones. We're tight, you hear me? We go out together, and we're going to come back together."

I felt uncomfortable when he said that they may not make it, but it was something in his eyes that told me he was convinced. I didn't try to figure it out. I knew if the Almighty was indeed with me, I did nothing to deserve it. There were so many of our men who never returned from the battlefield—men who had families and friends back home just like me, and with dreams that would never be fulfilled. I was no one special.

"Look, cut out the nonsense," I said. "We all are coming back, and not in a box!"

The uncertain look in their faces made me nervous.

I got up, slipped through the crowd into the back room and found a reel-to-reel player. I listened to the music until almost everyone had left.

That night, when I returned to my hooch, Connelly sat on my cot beside me. He still wanted to talk about the Triangle.

"If anything happens to me, promise me you'll see that my belongings get back to my family," he urged.

"Look, you gotta stop thinking like that," I said. "Nothing's gonna happen to you guys. I mean it, man."

Even after uttering those words, I couldn't shake my own uneasiness. I was afraid, too. Plenty afraid. I needed comfort just as much as anybody. But as his squad leader, I had to perform my duties like a Chaplain and keep my men calm.

A couple of weeks passed, and what we dreaded most was upon us. The 25th Infantry was encountering serious contact in the Iron Triangle. Our mission was to provide backup for them and search and destroy enemy targets. The gruesome stories were many. In time, I thought, we'd find out if the predictions were true. I hoped I'd live to tell about it.

We gathered our gear early the next morning and were alerted for liftoff. Before boarding the chopper to fly off into the wild yonder, I ordered my men to check the equipment and weapons to make sure we had enough ammo.

None of us talked much. It was unlike any other times we'd gone out. It was a silence that was rarely felt among us.

We could never get enough sleep. The most I'd gotten in two days was a couple of hours, not nearly enough. If we were in heavy conflict, we would get no sleep at all.

We boarded the chopper at 18:00. Our orders were to stay in the Trapezoid jungles for thirty days. The minute we landed, it felt like we'd dropped into the pit of hell as the darkness engulfed us.

After our LZ, we secured our position and mapped out our course. We walked about five clicks to our NDP. I was proud to be in The Big Red One. We had a reputation for being a very mobile army combat force in Vietnam.

We moved swiftly into position. The atmosphere was ominous. Even the jungle creatures seemed unusually quiet. Did they anticipate the attack as well?

I kissed Ava's picture. I knew my chances of coming out alive were slim. But, I held fast the thought I'd return to base and find good news.

Big Daddy and I went out to set up the trip mines and flares.

"When I leave on that bird, I don't want you to bullshit around and get messed up," he said. "You got to remember what you're living for. No one can love you like yourself and nobody can keep you alive like yourself."

I'd never seen such a look of deep sincerity as Big Daddy's face held. He seemed to be in deep thought as he set the mine and talked. Unlike other times when he'd said something to me, his voice was that of deep concern. He stood up and looked at me.

"You gotta stay strong," he said. "Abraham Lincoln said one time 'I had a friend that believed in me, and I didn't have the heart to let him down.' Don't let me down, friend."

I nodded and walked back with Big Daddy to our position. I pondered his words, still not knowing why he spoke to me in that way.

There had been no action that night. We'd gotten through the first day without any conflict. As soon as we had good visibility, we started to move.

I observed my men. As expected, each one moved about with grim looks on their faces. Connelly and Billy stayed close by my side. Connelly talked about his family a lot that day. I knew the thought of going into the Iron Triangle was getting to him, so I let him say all that was on his mind.

When day light broke, it was still quiet. A glimmer of the morning sunlight peeped through the tall, mangled foliage. Connelly sat with his legs crossed and head down. Billy fidgeted a lot with his hands. Big Daddy, with a tin can in his hand, came over and joined us. As always, he knew exactly what to say to spark a chuckle or two and boost morale. He joked about his upbringing and the daring things he did as a teen. It was only small talk to get our minds off the mission. I stared at this tall, dark-skinned man who talked a lot with his mouth full of food.

He scraped the bottom of his tin can and swallowed hard, washing down the rest of his rations with the last bit of water from his canteen. Then he showed us how he cleans his can with his tongue. There was not one particle left in Big Daddy's ration can. He wiped his mouth with his handkerchief and chuckled. "Now, let's go kill us some damn gooks!" he said. He looked at us with a cocked smile and winked as if he knew something that we didn't know

I couldn't figure Big Daddy out. He couldn't be immune to the conditions, I thought. No one second-guessed him or questioned whether or not he'd panic in the Triangle. It was remarkable to watch him.

I tried striking a conversation with Billy. I could clearly see turmoil on his face. Before we left base for the Triangle, I noticed how clumsy he appeared. He dropped things several times and struggled to get in his boots. I remembered my conversation with him back at base camp, and I reminded him of it.

"We're going in together and we'll come back together," I said, emphasizing each word and looking him in his eyes. But deep inside, I knew he didn't believe me. At that point, I wondered if I believed myself.

Billy said, "Like I said, me and Connelly . . . we don't know a thing about the man upstairs. We never hear you cussing or swearing and you always have that black book with you. That makes us know you'll make it."

"For the last time, I'm no saint," I said, adamantly. "It's just that my mother put the fear of God in us when we were growing up. That forbade us from using his name in vain or words she thought were profane. So, I feared her,not God."

I pulled out my Bible and held the small book to Billy.

"She made me bring this," I continued. "I'm glad she did, because it's the only safe place for my pictures."

Billy smiled.

"I know nothing about that book," I went on to say. "I got most of this stuff from my mother, and I sleep with it to remind the devil who she is."

That made him chuckle. It was good to see them smiling.

Around midday, the sun had peaked. Sweat poured down my chest and my back. My green T-shirt was badly soiled, clinging to my hot, damp skin. Wetting my handkerchief with water from my canteen, I pressed the damp cloth on my forehead and neck. In seconds, the cloth had dried from the blazing sun.

I checked my jacket pocket to see if Ava's picture with her posing in her skimpy bathing suit was still where I'd tucked it. It was there, wrapped in the wrinkled plastic protective sheets I'd made for it.

Exhausted and hardly able to manage the rough paths, I struggled with the other men, fighting my way through the bush of tangled vines. I was swatting mosquitoes by the dozen. The sun sucked our energy like mosquitoes drawing our blood. I had a canteen of water and a canteen of booze, and neither helped much. I sipped warm water from my canteen and almost gagged. My throat was dry and scratchy, making it painful to talk. Every few minutes, I drew a mouthful of spit and swallowed hard, trying to get enough saliva to wet my throat. My body was begging for rest, but the mission was not nearly over.

We were in the bush for thirty long days without conflict. Then, we got news that the mission was over. At last, I thought, we were headed back to base without the fierce battle we'd expected. There was a new level of energy from all of us when we got the news. We started clowning around, giving handshakes, and gathering our gear as fast as we could. I looked at Connelly and Billy. They looked relaxed and calm, now.

We started moving toward our PZ. I felt mighty good. We had dodged the bullet with experiencing the terrible stories told at base about the Iron Triangle. I was excited, too, thinking about the letter from Howard that may be waiting for me at base. We were the lucky ones, we thought. But, to our dismay, we were wrong.

CHAPTER 11

We were only a click away from our PZ, when suddenly gun blasts hit from every direction.

"Cover . . . down!" Big Daddy yelled.

We fell to the ground. Without any signs or indications, we'd walked into a U-shaped ambush, one of the worst. We had no idea Charlie was waiting for us.

Shots were coming so heavily that we hardly had time to take cover. The enemy must have been on our radio frequency and discovered our location.

I heard a soldier yell, "This shit's hit the fan!"

It was obvious we'd walked into a death trap. We were pinned down with rifle fire, RPGs, and rocket launchers coming at us. This time, we were like sitting ducks, frozen with nowhere to run or hide. The unimaginable, horrible nightmare of what we thought we'd dodged was staring us in our faces.

Fear surged through me. For the first time, I could taste death. It felt like I was in an action-packed movie —except there were no cameras and no director to yell "cut."

I knew to do as I was instructed, and do it quickly. Billy fed ammo into my MG. I fired back hard and steady. One guy fell from a blast a few yards from me. Fragments of flesh shot into the air and landed on my face and chest.

After heavy exchange of gunfire, we moved back and got behind small, uprooted trees that didn't provide much covering. The Viet Cong had us trapped right in their KZ. They were well dug in, and we were easy targets.

For a moment, I didn't know which way to move. BOOM! Another explosive hit and before I knew what was coming, my helmet was knocked off by shrapnel.

The jungle was so thick that fighting in the daytime was the same as fighting at night. I couldn't see anything. Unimaginable agonizing sounds hit my ears from men screaming in pain. I was powerless to help them.

Within minutes, I'd planned my own funeral. I wanted no long eulogy, just a simple prayer would do. I figured the military would provide a decent ceremonial burial. I didn't want people dropping by with food and flowers, telling my parents what a wonderful friend I'd been when they had not bothered to write me. I imagined my father trying to be strong for my mother as she wept at the graveside with the sound of "Taps" as my rest in peace tribute. The volleys, customarily fired over the grave, would send children clinging to their parents and babies crying.

I signaled my men to keep low. Another explosion hit nearby. Heavy smoke like dark thunderous clouds ascended into the air. Seconds later, I heard someone call my name. It was very loud and clear. I thought that it might have been my lieutenant's voice. I commanded Billy and Connelly to stay down. Hurriedly, I maneuvered my way through the jungle, stepping over our men. I couldn't tell whether they were dead, or if they still had breath in their bodies. I stumbled blindly along as shots whistled by me.

When I found my lieutenant, he was lying on his back on the ground. He couldn't speak, not even a whisper.

A huge pool of blood encompassed his head. At first, I couldn't tell where he'd been hit or how severe he'd been wounded. I moved his head and blood spewed from his neck down onto his shoulders and arms like water from a faucet.

I pulled him to my chest and pressed my thumb into the hole in the side of his neck trying to control blood flow. His mouth was slightly parted with blood oozing from one corner. I pulled my bandana to plug the hole in his throat, but it was no use. Blood was spurting out much too fast. In seconds, he drew his last breath. I watched as his eyes sank into his head. His eyelids closed and he went limp in my arms. I thought I was in a nightmare and that I would wake up any moment. This is not happening. It can't be, I thought. I clutched him in my arms and rocked him like a mother cradling her baby boy.

All of a sudden, I heard a crackling sound. Before I could take cover, a loud explosion erupted. Flying shrapnel caught me in the side and arm. It felt as if the force of high voltage wires had struck me. My body went numb at first. Then a piercing, knife-like pain ripped through my flesh. A hot, dull burning sensation ran up and down my upper left arm and side. I saw the blood gush through my shirt. There was no time, however, to attend to my wounds. I had to get back to my men.

Trying to block out the increasing pain, I clutched my side, left my lieutenant and struggled back to my position. As I threaded my way to my post, the firing ceased from enemy line.

When I got to my men, I was thunderstruck. What I saw looked like a huge crime scene, only ten times worse. My squad was completely annihilated. Either RPG rounds or a rocket had hit the area. My two buddies, Connelly and Billy,had taken a serious blow from the explosives. It looked like a pack of ferocious wolves had fought violently to claim them. Their faces were hardly recognizable, and blood had covered every inch of their bodies. I looked over at Billy. He had taken a blast to his side. There was huge gash, exposing his raw insides. Connelly was lying not far from him. His twisted limbs had been separated from his body.

I turned aside and saw one of my comrades lying on his back. His stomach was split open, and his bloody guts were pushed outward. Not far from him was another one of my men. He'd lost half of his face from severe burns. Debris from the explosives covered his uniform.

Afar off, I could hear moans and groans from my fallen comrades as they yelled for medics. I sought frantically for my machine gun. When I found it, the barrel had melted completely out of shape by the intense heat from a rocket or whatever hit that area.

One of our men who survived staggered up behind me.

"Son of a bitch!" His eyes stretched with terror.

He stood alongside me, looking upon our fallen men on the cruel earth underneath them. In every direction, bodies were splattered on the ground like meat in a slaughterhouse. I checked all of them to see if they were alive. Not one soldier was breathing. I moved slowly around body parts and looked upon disfigured faces with blood—so much blood, too much blood mingled together.

I felt like a walking dead man. I stood in one spot horrified at the most brutal atrocities I'd ever encountered. I wanted to scream, but the emotional pain was too great, forbidding any audible sounds. My knees gave way and I dropped to the ground and wept. Death had its victory over us.

In a clearing, the medics rushed wounded men on litters to the choppers. Some yelled out, "Medic! Medic!"

There were four medics to a company. With a company of our size, the number of casualties was more than our medics could handle. I pulled up and stood to let them know I could walk. Sadly, I could only take a couple of steps before pain rushed through my arms and side. I knew I'd lost a lot of blood and more gushed out with my every move. When I felt strong enough, I limped onward.

Turning around, I took one last look at the fragmented remains of Billy and Connelly. In less than three minutes, I had lost my two good buddies. They had met me halfway across the bridge of racial prejudice and made me realize there were some good white people in the world. I didn't think I could ever have two white men as close buddies, but they proved me wrong. Now they were gone. Their words came back to me. "Carolina, if anyone makes it out of here, you will." I then realized what they had been feeling all along was real.

The tall, thick foliage made it almost impossible to see, but I pressed forward. After I had limped a few yards away from Connelly and Billy, I tripped over a fallen tree and fell to the ground. As I struggled to get up, my eyes fell upon another soldier. He was sprawled on his back with bullet wounds to nearly every part of his body. I felt his pulse. He was alive, but he was in serious condition. Unable to carry him, I left and searched for someone, anyone who was in good enough condition to help. But there was not a man standing, and the medics were working fiercely to keep each one alive. Each one I passed alive was in the same condition as I was—weak and bleeding profusely.

I looked down. My torso was covered with deep red, warm blood that was drying fast from the heat. When I tried to remove my T-shirt to examine my wounds, the fabric was glued firmly to my side where the blood was drying, fast. It pained me to raise my arms or make even the slightest movement.

I limped my way across the jungle, got into a clearing and dropped to the ground with several other wounded men. A few seconds later, I looked up. What was in front of me was more disturbing than the casualties I'd seen a few yards behind. Big Daddy came staggering out of the thickets. He'd been hit, hard. I couldn't tell where he'd been shot, but I suspected he'd taken a blow to the head. A thick patch of blood covered his forehead and ran down both sides of his face. His entire chest was drenched in blood and debris. Nothing was visible except his eyes. The only way I recognized him was by his stocky physique and his big hands as he walked like a zombie into the clearing.

I had an insurmountable urge to get to him, but I was hurting too badly to walk. I don't believe Big Daddy ever saw me. He kept walking with the most determined strides I'd ever seen on someone in that condition. He stumbled, but he never fell.

The medics grabbed him, but they practically had to force him to lie onto the litter. He kept pointing his finger to the other wounded men, telling the medics to assist them before they helped him. Each time I'd watch him rescue wounded men, one at a time, he never seemed to care about himself at all. He carried them like a shepherd bearing his wounded sheep. I wasn't sure what a brave soldier was, until that day— when I saw him nearly dead and still giving orders to the medics to take care of the other men before they attended to him.

I looked on as white soldiers carried wounded black comrades over their shoulders, and black soldiers helped medics lift helpless, nearly lifeless white men to safety. In the war, there were no segregated toilets, lunch counters, or churches. We were neck to neck in the thicket of the jungle, in trenches, rice patties, and small dwellings at base camp. There was no division. No time for discriminating. In the states, I'd seen natural catastrophes and other kind of disasters bringing people together of all races. But it was different in war. We were one big band of brothers—black, white, Asians, and Latinos—caring for each man like he was our own flesh. We had one purpose and that was to watch each other's backs and try to get every man home to safety.

It wasn't long before we heard the glorious sound of our birds, the 2nd and 16th Rangers of the Big Red Division, coming in the blue skies to reinforce us. Moments later, I heard a loud roar. Our fighter jets burst into sight. They were there to waste the area. We could see, from our position, our F15 fighter jet covering the area. The highly reactive poisonous spray was so powerful that it could burn the skin off a human being in a matter of seconds before it reached him. The blanket of the destructive substance came down thick and heavy. It looked like someone spraying acid on an insect mound.

The medics loaded the choppers with the wounded and dead. When I boarded, I felt lightheaded and buried my head between my knees. Seconds later, my eyes fell on a soldier we called "the professor" because of his brilliant intellect. There was a hallow look in his eyes as if he wasn't sure where he was. At least he made it out, I thought. I knew he was fighting not far from Connelly and Billy. I never expected to see him alive.

We were silent. I looked over at the three men in the platoon that survived without any injuries. The faces of the two white soldiers were deeply blushed, and the black soldier's face looked washed out. The severely wounded were groaning. Some had tears streaming down their cheeks. The dead men were placed in body bags and stacked on top of each other. Some were placed right next to me.

One man sat with his head tucked between his knees. He rocked back and forth. When he looked up, his eyes were locked in his head. I knew he was in extreme mental anguish and would need immediate psychiatric attention when we got back to base camp. Death, hell and destruction had taken a toll on all of us.

I studied the other men on the chopper who were strong enough to sit upright and wondered what was going on in their heads. Like me, they were young men who were fresh out of high school. They'd been forced to witness horrible things that would stay with them for the rest of their lives. Every guy in my platoon had been drafted. None of us were volunteers. The professor had a teaching degree he'd just begun to use before the draft. Many of the men in our unit were educated. Some had degrees from a university or trade school.

Perhaps I missed the logic of having men drafted into the war with obvious careers ahead of them. I'd heard the army's philosophical idea of pulling professionals first. The logic was they'd be the ones who had a reason to fight hard in order to get back home. Those with no dreams or aspirations or little education were most likely to give up easier, they said. I begged to differ. All of us wanted to get back home.

I rested my head against the hard wall of the chopper while thoughts continued to race in my head. I reflected on the war with certainty most of us had no clue as to why we, Americans, were fighting. From what I could understand, US troops were sent to prevent a communist takeover of South Vietnam. I knew only that much and, quite frankly, I didn't care to know any more. My comrades had just died in a gruesome fight. They had families back home. The heartache was awaiting them. There were the severely wounded, some who would never walk again or hold a loved one in his arms. If awards were waiting, they were for heroes as the military would see it. But, as we combatants saw it, we heroes were only fortunate survivors. Acts of courage to a soldier is the loyalty he has for his fellow comrade.

I kept heaving like I was going to throw up. I wanted to burst into tears, but the most I could do was hold my side and groan.

I meditated on the attack. I knew I'd seen a divine intervention in my life. From looking at my lieutenant in his weak condition, I didn't see how he had enough strength to call me. He hardly had enough breath to exhale. The voice I heard was loud and strong.

It was a miracle I'd escaped the ambush. In only two or three minutes, I'd left my post and returned to find all of my men except three, dead. I was bewildered as to why my life was spared while Connelly and Billy who fought shoulder to shoulder with me didn't make it. Could it have been the voice of God beckoning me? And if so, why me?

After that fight in the Triangle, I understood clearly why American citizens back home were protesting against the White House's rationale for keeping us in the country. It was unethical, inhumane and ludicrous to be in South Vietnam.

My perspective about war or conflicts of any kind has always been that we use less physical force and apply proper thought to resolutions. Issues can be resolved in a friendly manner. I remember somewhere reading a statement Benjamin Franklin made. It was something like he'd hoped mankind who considered themselves responsible creatures would have enough sense to settle their differences without cutting throats. His statement made a lot of sense to me. This war did not. And my hope of ever returning home, of ever seeing Ava, again, was fading fast.

CHAPTER 12

We landed at headquarters. My hospitals of my unit, The Big Red One, were completely full, so they had to medevac me to the 25th Infantry Division hospital. It was a stab of reality as to how horrible the fight was when I passed so many men in wheelchairs and others against the wall, still bleeding and waiting for help. The medics carried me on a stretcher to the back of the room. I saw a long table that looked like it was used for operating. Beside it was a small cart holding utensils perfectly aligned on the edge of a tray. There was a strong odor of dead flesh coming from the beds where men had bled and perhaps died.

A short, blonde headed nurse jerked the sheets off one bed where the pungent smell was coming and placed fresh linen on it. She signaled for me to lie down.

"The doctor will be here soon," she said, as she helped me onto the bed.

I looked at the men on the row of cots in front of me. Their faces were feeble and wrought with pain. The doctors and nurses kept running from stretcher to stretcher, calling for assistance. I thought about the sacrifice the medical staff was making for us. They were our angels from heaven, and we had no way of showing our appreciation.

I ran my fingers up and down my arm to make sure it wasn't going numb. I hurt all over and couldn't tell what part of my body was damaged the most.

I looked at my hands, still bloody from the fight. My own blood caught between my fingers was now mingled with my lieutenant's blood. I felt my face and started to pull meat particles I'd caught from my fallen buddies who'd been hit not too far from me.

I looked around at a few men I recognized from base camp. Some were passed out, undergoing surgery. Others lay motionless on cots, waiting for attention.

In less than ten minutes after I got there, another group of soldiers arrived. The nurses and doctors carried trays of supplies as they scrambled to get to the most critical ones. By the looks of things, quite a few of us were hurt. I couldn't image how many of our men were dead.

Each time I tried to speak, my teeth chattered. I asked the nurse what was happening to me.

"Your body is in shock," she said.

I could tell by the sound of her voice that she wasn't up for conversation. She pulled a thin cover over my feet and walked off. A few minutes later, the room got quiet. The silence was eerie. I wasn't sure if the wounded stopped groaning because the medication had started working or if they had left this world all together.

It took about an hour before a white medical doctor approached my bedside. He introduced himself as Dr. Burns. Then he lifted my arm and proceeded to examine the large, bloody gashes.

"What about my men?" I asked, as I struggled to sit up. He looked at me without saying a word and started ripping off the side of my shirt with a blade. I watched him bury his eyes in my wounds. I'm not sure if he was deliberately not answering me or if he just hadn't gotten around to a question and answer session.

"You're pretty damn lucky," he said.

He became engrossed in his observations of my wounds. He then pulled a small flashlight and followed the gash down my left side.

"It's ugly . . . but it could be worse," he said, as he placed my left arm back down. With his eyes locked into a fixed position, he frowned.

"There are pieces of shrapnel we have to get out now," he said.

"How are the other men?" I demanded. I coughed and a pain shot through my body like a rocket. I grabbed my side and took in a deep breath.

"Did Big Daddy make it?" I asked, groaning.

Dr. Burns remained silent. Then I was sure he was deliberately ignoring me. He stared at my wounded left arm with a serious look as though what he saw was of great concern. Within a short time, a different nurse approached the bed with a syringe.

"I'll be back," Dr. Burns said. He walked swiftly away.

I looked into the face of the young white woman who wore a smile on her face.

"I'm Dana," she said. She winked at me as she introduced herself. I felt relieved that she seemed different from the first nurse. Her touch was warm and gentle.

"You're going to be just fine," she said, squeezing my hand. She slipped a pillow under my arm. "This will help reduce the blood flow."

She laughed and said. "My mother who is an old school pro told me that. I didn't learn that in nursing school."

The pillow under my arm did make it throb less. She reached for clean white bandages. I felt a warm solution on my forehead and then the dabbing of a cool cloth. She ran her fingers across my forehead and gazed at my head.

"Looks like you got some bad cuts here," she said.

"Yeah, I figured it happened when my helmet was knocked off," I said. I tried to sit up in the bed. Dana grabbed my arm to assist me.

"You don't need to move a lot," she said."Look, I just want to know why Dr. Burns didn't answer me about my men," I said. "I have a good friend . . . like a father to me. His name is George, but we call him Big Daddy. I just want to know if he's all right."

"Dr. Burns never talks to a soldier about the wounded or dead," she said. "He leaves that to the commanding officers. He's all about his work. Any talk unrelated to what he's doing is not a subject he deems urgent. Some other soldiers find it quite disturbing as well. But that's Dr. Burns."

"That's good to know," I said."I thought all of you white people in here didn't like black soldiers."

Dana laughed.

"No, that's not me. I was raised by a black woman. She was a good friend of my mother's."

Just as she finished wrapping my head, Dr. Burns returned in his white jacket with sterile gloves and supplies on a cart.

"Relax, soldier," he said. "You're going to feel some pressure."

He took a swab from the tray that had been soaked in a solution and started probing my flesh.

"Oh, please stop!" I said.

It wasn't pressure, it was indescribable pain that ran through my arm and traveled all the way to my back. A butcher would've done better with the procedure, I thought. I balled my fist and tried to bare it, but the pain worsened. If he was using the swab to numb me, I couldn't tell.

I struggled on the bed to get up. Dana held me down and signaled for another person in medical garb. He immediately held my arm to keep me from moving. Another thrust of the blade found my open wound. Dana squeezed my hand. My eyes squint shut. I groaned and gripped the side of the bed. Then I saw Dana pull a syringe from the tray.

"Hold tight," Dana said. She found my vein. I felt a slight pinch and she was done.

"What did you give me?" I asked.

"Something to ease the pain," she said.

"It's not working," I said.

"Give it time," she said.

"I feel like I'm gonna throw up," I said.

She grabbed a pan and put it under my chin. I was delirious. Another stabbing pain went across my arm.

"Give me more," I pleaded.

"Another dose and you'll be dead," Dr. Burns said. He backed off a bit and gave me time to get my breath. Dana tried placing a white cloth over my mouth.

"Bite hard," she said.

Dr. Burns turned to Dana. "He's lost a lot of blood."

He started speaking in medical terms, describing my condition to her. I didn't understand what they were discussing. I didn't care. All I wanted was to be put to sleep for a long, long time.

I tried to think of something pleasant. Ava came to mind, but I pushed the thought of her away. It hurt even more to think about her. I was tired, and I wanted nothing more than to go home to the good old USA. From the day I arrived, it had been one hellish thing after another happening to me.

I turned my thoughts to my family to take my mind off the pain. I missed them badly. I had three sisters—Imogene, Shelly, Rachel, and five brothers Leroy, Thomas, Frank, Rufus, and Raymond.

I thought about my brother, Frank. I knew if he was in my position, his words wouldn't have been pleasant. He was quiet, but he had a high temper. He was the opposite of my middle brother, Leroy, whose character was meek and mild. Personality-wise, I fell somewhere in between the two of them.

I remembered my father's expression one day when he had us all together at his birthday dinner. He told us how proud he was of all of us, especially the ones who had athletic skills like him. My brother, Thomas, was an all-conference football player in high school. Frank played football, and Rufus was a wrestling champion. I was an all-around athlete with potentials of a professional baseball career. Although Leroy and Rachel were commended for their track running skills they got from my father, no one could outrun him.

Another pain shot through my body. I cringed while I held tightly to the edge of my bed. "Focus! Focus on the family!" I said in my mind.

I thought about Imogene and Shelly who didn't have one athletic bone in them, but they both played a unique role in the family. Imogene was the one we all consulted when we needed sound advice. Shelly beat us all with smarts and wit. And when we needed a laugh, the comedian in her could always make that happen. When I introduced Ava to my family, she instantly fit in with them. In fact, she was such part of our reunions that people other than my family thought we were married. Despite our quarrels from time to time, our family was one great big ball of fun.

I watched closely as Dana and Dr. Burns attended to my wounds.

Loud groans came from a new soldier that had just arrived. His cot was not too far from me. From what I could see from my bed, both of his legs had been blown off. The medics worked frantically with him. After a few minutes, there were no sounds at all.

Dr. Burns placed the blade into my side. My hands trembled, and my body shook as he dug into my flesh. For a split second, I envisioned my arm in a swing or paralyzed.

After a few seconds, the pain lessened. I heard metal hitting the tray. Dana stood over me with a look of compassion. I felt like a little boy, wanting to hear her say, "I know it's hard now, but everything is going to be all right."

Dr. Burns was about to gouge more, but another physician, presumed to be his boss, walked over and took a look at my wounds.

"Close him up," he ordered. "Any more digging might cause damage."

He was my angel, I thought. I watched Dr. Burns place his instruments on the tray and walk away with the other physician.

Suddenly, my entire side went numb. Whatever Dana gave me finally worked. I don't remember much after that as I faded into darkness. When I woke hours later, Dana came to my bedside. She was smiling as she carried a small pouch with her.

"It's time for your meds," she said. She pulled a tiny pill from the bag and handed it to me with a cup of water.

"What's this?" I asked.

"An antibiotic," she said, in a cheerful voice. She pulled out another pill and handed it to me.

"If you still feel nauseated, this will help," she said.

I looked around the room. The other wounded soldiers seemed to be resting fairly well.

"Did they have surgery?" I asked.

She shook her head. "No. They came in for some stitches. But one guy came in with eighteen bullet holes in him." She nodded to her right. "He's right over there, still breathing. And from the looks of it, the doctor says he's gonna make it.

"That's a miracle," I said. "I saw him in the bush and never thought he'd live. I've seen a lot of miracles in this war, but I've never seen anything like that guy.

She reached for my arm and took my blood pressure.

"We got to work on stabilizing your pressure, she said. "But it's better than when you arrived."

She patted my arm. "You're going to be fine, though. They are letting you go back to base. So get all the rest you can."

She pulled the covers over me. "And you were talking out of your head for awhile," she said.

"What did I say?" I asked.

"I couldn't make it out," she said.

She walked over to a table close by and came back with Ava's picture in her hand. It was still wrapped in the plastic I'd put it in.

"I pulled this from your shirt pocket," she said. "It was pretty bloody. I tried to disinfect it as much as possible."

I raised my head from the pillow and took the picture from her hand. It was unharmed in the plastic, except for the edges that got roughed up during the fight. I couldn't do anything but stare at the picture. I was so glad that it remained safe.

"No one was supposed to see this," I said, as I gazed at the photo. "I promised Ava."

Dana whizzed around.

"Ava! That's what you were saying," she said. "You mumbled a lot. I thought you were saying 'Abel', you know, Adam and Eve's son. I wondered if I should be concerned." She laughed and left the room.

I shut my eyes and pulled Ava's picture to my chest. I was able to turn over in bed for the first time by myself. The room was quiet. I didn't want to go back to sleep, but I was out in a second as soon as Dana left.

I had slept well into the afternoon. When I woke, I could feel Dr. Burns' cool hands on my arm.

"Sgt. Dula, I need you to wake up for me." I heard him saying.

The sedative had worked so well that I could hardly open my eyes. I felt if I didn't have anything to help me, my body would have eventually sedated itself from the pain.

"The shrapnel are not as accessible as we'd hoped," he said. "Some are deep. There are some lodged in your arm that's too risky. They're too close to a main nerve. If I proceed with the surgery, I could damage you permanently. At all cost, we will avoid that."

I was thankful he didn't say I would lose my arm. I was all right about the shrapnel staying in my body as long as I was able to keep my arm.

"You should be able to go back to the field," he said. "However, I want you to stay out for a couple of weeks."

He left me and walked over to another soldier's bed.

Dana placed her arm underneath me and helped me turn. "Try to lie still, now," she said.

Dr. Burns nodded to Dana and she left quickly behind him. I wanted to ask about my men and Big Daddy, but she didn't give me a chance. No one said a word to me about the attack.

A medic walked by with a clipboard. It looked like he was counting the number of men in the room. I questioned him about Big Daddy. His eyes raced up and down on the chart of survivals. He then shook his head slowly.

"I don't see that name here with the others," he said.

"Look, again," I urged. "George Dowd's his real name."

He looked doubtful and he stared at the chart, again moving his finger slowly down the list of names. I strained to see the piece of paper. He stopped at the bottom.

"No luck. There's nothing close to that name," he said, and he moved on.

Hot as the evening was, a chill came over me. But, it wasn't from the atmosphere in the room. I felt confused and guilty. Why did my men die, and I lived? I felt like I'd failed Connelly and Billy by promising them they would return.

Loneliness swept over me as my mind drifted back to Ava. I wanted to see her more than anything. I knew by now she must be sick of Jerome. He had the appearance of a male chauvinist, someone she'd soon get tired of seeing, I thought.

I needed to hear good news, the news I had long waited for. I had my hopes up high that mail would be waiting for me when I got back to camp. Things would take a turn for the better, I kept telling myself. Just don't give up.

I was released from the hospital the next day. I dreaded going back to the base and seeing the empty beds in my hooch, but I knew I couldn't stay in the medical facility. There were too many critically wounded men coming in who needed a bed.

I was flown back to my base camp with my arm in a sling. The pain had eased, but it never stopped. I was afraid to take a lot of pain killers. In fact, I was more fearful of getting hooked on pain relievers than becoming an alcoholic.

When I got to my unit, the 1st Division Headquarters of the Big Red One, it was just like I thought it would be, quiet and morbid. I greeted the remaining eight men out of the twenty-five who lived with me in my quarters. Although I was happy to see them, it was a sad feeling walking past empty cots once occupied by men who'd become like family. They were men who didn't deserve what happened in the Triangle. Connelly and Billy had not yet turned 21, the legal age of drinking in America, yet the war gave them their first drink. I thought about the times they talked about their future careers, school, marriage, and children. Together, we'd huddled in trenches, told jokes that were only funny to the ones who felt like laughing, shared our rations and drank water from the same canteen. We'd trampled the rice patties and watched each other's backs in the jungle.

A few minutes after I arrived, my sergeant called me into his office at headquarters.

"I am proud to award you these," he said. "You have earned these for your outstanding actions in the field—the Purple Heart and Bronze Star."

I wasn't thinking about awards or accolades. There was nothing on my mind except my men, particularly Connelly and Billy, who weren't so lucky.

When you listen to a combat's story, it all boils down to one thing—we were a band of brothers. And when we bled, everyone's blood was the same color, red. In all the races, crying and laughter share the same language, and when death comes, it has no preference. I thought about our officers who would have the formidable task of contacting family members, gathering belongings to be shipped home, and returning letters that never got opened.

It had been a fierce battle, but none of our fallen men went down without giving the enemy all the force of combat that was possible. Weak and wounded, they staggered forward, some almost crawling as they pursued with determination. Pressing forward and numbed by fatigue, they fought on gallantly. No one ever would've guessed by seeing them fight, they had gone days with hardly an ounce of sleep.

I got back to my hooch and stared at the men who were left. They sat with looks of despair and grief. I found my cot and sat down. One of the soldiers who survived the attack saw me. He got up and pulled me into a big hug. His countenance was a mixture of sadness and joy.

"Good to see you," he said.

"Same here," I said.

"We thought we had lost you," he said. "There was one guy shot about eighteen times.

"Yeah, I know," I said. "I saw him with holes in every part of his body."

"Well, he lived, believe it or not," he said.

"Where's Big Daddy?" I asked. "Is he all right?"

He nodded. "He was shot up pretty bad. I don't know his condition, but as soon as he got to headquarters, he was medevaced to Japan for treatment since his time is short."

I dropped down on my cot in relief. Big Daddy was still alive. I walked over to Connelly's and Billy's empty bunks and held my eyes to the family portraits over their beds. Connelly's voice came back to me.

"Don't forget, Carolina," he said. "If anything happens to me, I want you to get my things back home."

Their talk of dying was right, and I was wrong. I never thought I'd ever cry over any white men, but I couldn't control the tears. We were a bridge for each other. Their footprints were on my shoulders, and my footprints would be buried with them.

I grew more and more despondent of the war. I wanted nothing to do with the political propaganda of aiding people I knew nothing about. It was inconceivable for me to believe that the war was fought for what the White House officials called acts of humanitarianism. But in reality, I asked myself isn't that what the Negro ancestry had struggled and fought for and had never quite obtained it in the name of humanitarianism? And these innocent civilians of Vietnam, my fellow comrades and officers were dying because of what? Surely, not to save humanity, I thought.

I looked over at Connelly's bed. At the top of his cot was a newspaper clipping he'd saved. His sister had sent it to him from the states. I read it that day. The Secretary of State had said in the article, "We are in Vietnam to help establish a climate in which people and governments will let other peoples and governments alone." I guess the clipping reminded him of the reason he was there.

A soldier sat down on the cot in front of me. He didn't say a word. The silence was a treasure. We needed no words, no statements. Our hearts understood the language of our souls.

During the night, I had an overwhelming feeling of guilt. There was a great sense of failure on my part. I couldn't save my lieutenant as I watched him die in my arms. I felt guilty that I couldn't help Big Daddy, the bravest man I'd ever seen.

I sat on my cot, unable to close my eyes. My mind wouldn't shut down. I thought I was in a terrible nightmare. But when I looked at the empty cots and continued peeling flesh of my fallen comrades off my shirt, it was far from a dream.

CHAPTER 13

The mail arrived. It had been several weeks since we'd gotten the last bundle. As usual, I stood in line with much anticipation. Could this be my lucky day? Could this be the day that I kiss despair and hopelessness goodbye? Would I get the letter I was waiting for?

A soldier handed me a stack of envelopes. I stepped out of line and thumbed through the pile. I got one from my cousin, another one from a girl I went to school with, one from my mother. And then, my eyes fell on the return address of the last envelope. Instead of a letter from Howard, it was clearly Ava's handwriting I was seeing. My heart started pounding, wildly. It was something I least expected, and I didn't know what to do. I tucked the other letters under my arm, and rushed back to my hooch to read in private the words that were going to make my day.

I hurled the rest of the mail on my cot and slit the envelop open. Then, without any warning, I read the lines that I least expected. No one could have prepared me for what I saw on the ripped notebook sheet of paper written in the handwriting for which I was so accustomed. The first line in the letter made blood rush to my head, and I felt faint and sick.

Dear Ken,

You may be surprised to hear from me, but I talked with Howard and I don't want you to think we'll ever get back together. It was too hard for me to wait for you not knowing if you would ever come back. I'm sorry I hurt you. Right now, I have future plans with someone else, and I don't want to see you again. I wish you the best.

Ava

I held my chest and sat down on a crate. Several minutes passed before I could put the letter down. Insurmountable grief swept over me like a heat wave, and everything around me seemed nonexistent. Even the voices of the men not far from me were muffled and sounded far away.

I'd been in a horrendous battle, the worst since I'd arrived in South Vietnam. I'd lost nearly all of my men, including my best buddies and assistant gunners, Connelly and Billy; my lieutenant died in my arms; I watched Big Daddy stumbling through the bushes with blood thicker than mud from his head to his midsection; my own body was nearly destroyed by shrapnel wounds so deeply I could hardly move. I crawled over fragmented bodies and disjointed limbs from men who I ate with and laughed with; and into thick foliage, I'd dodged bullets and incoming mortar. Particles of lead were still in my flesh from flying shrapnel. I thought I had experienced the worst, but it was Ava's letter that ripped my soul to pieces and took my will to live.

She'd become my life. I'd carried her in my heart for days, weeks, and months. I took her to the trenches. She lay next to me in the rice patties. It was she who followed me to the fields each time I went. It was her sweet fragrance that tortured me and her face that disturbed my rest when I closed my eyes. I'd held her in my memories with thoughts of the wonderful times we had together. I heard her laughter, her words of encouragement; the sweet caresses of her soft hands exploring my body when we made love—all of which kept me alive. I was almost there, right there at the top of my mountain when I saw her envelope.

Sadly, the demons of my soul had won, leaving me in a valley of hopelessness. I loved her more than life, itself.

I'm not sure how long Brody had been standing over me, talking. Suddenly, I felt his hand on my shoulder. I looked up into his face.

"Carolina, did you hear me?" I heard him say. "Are you coming with us? We're going to the village and get some chicks!"

I stared at him with my lips slightly parted. My distress must have shown. He stopped smiling.

"Not good, right?" he said.

I was speechless. He patted me on the shoulder.

"Wanna talk?" he asked.

I shook my head slowly. He stood for a few seconds.

"Are you sure you're okay?" he asked.

I nodded and turned away. My eyes burned from trying to hold back tears. Finally, he got the point and walked off, leaving me alone.

"Catch up with me later," he called over his shoulder.

I was by myself, embracing the silence. My father's words when I was a kid came to me. "Big boys don't cry." He had said a real man should show strength and integrity; he should hold his head up high and carry on the affairs of his life with dignity.

But I wasn't my father. And, in this case he was wrong. Big boys do cry. Uncontrollable tears streamed down my cheeks. For a moment, I thought Howard had betrayed me, and I was angry with him. But then again, I could see why he wouldn't have written me, letting me know Ava never wanted to see me. He didn't have the heart. Friends don't hurt friends.

What went so terribly wrong? Did someone play a dirty trick on me? The tone of the letter sounded nothing like the sweet, caring and loving voice I left behind.

I starred at the letter through blurred vision. All the hope I had left was now washed away like a tidal wave.

I crawled in a fetal position and held my chest trying to keep it from hurting. Unfortunately, there are no pain killers or healing salve for heartache—only time and grace from heaven could make a difference. Each time I thought about Ava's words "I never want to see you, again," written on the notebook paper, I sobbed harder. It felt like I had been lowered into a cold, bottomless pit engulfed by a thousand midnights without anything to grab onto to keep from descending. Until now, I never really believed anyone could die of a broken heart. I could no longer feel any kind of emotion, good or bad.

It didn't help me, but I pulled out an old letter of Ava's from underneath my cot. Pieces of the worn edges fell off from multiple readings. I read a line I'd circled, written so carefully with her small fingers. "I will be waiting for you when you return." Did she know how much I believed her? Maybe she was never in love with me. That thought sent a sharp, throbbing pain down the side of my arm. The wound felt fresh all over, again.

For an hour, I stayed there and recalled pleasant memories of Ava. My mind played back the first time she told me that she was in love with me. She cuddled next to me on her sofa. I could hear her giggle. I could almost feel the night air at the lake as if I were there on the green grass, listening to her voice and watching the swans make their way to the edge and back into the water.

I thought about the first time we made love at Lovers Cove. She was more than wonderful that night. I was crazy to think another man wouldn't try to make his move on her. She loved me. I was sure of it. I tried to comfort myself with that thought.

Finally, I decided to go to the club and get as quickly to the bar as I could. It was nearly midnight when I joined my comrades at the NCO. The jukebox blasted Freda Payne's song, "Bring the Boys Back Home."

I don't know why we tortured ourselves, but it seemed as if that song was our companion. We couldn't get enough of playing it.

Smoke and the smell of liquor filled the place. I stood at the door and inhaled the odor. Everything about the club felt good to me.

When I got to the bar, Brody was sitting there. I walked over to him. He patted a place for me to sit.

"You look like death," he said. His eyes were glassy and wild. He pushed a bottle of whiskey to me. I'd never drunk anything other than a beer and the spiked punch at my going away party. But, I felt I needed something to dull the ache inside, so I took the bottle and reached for a glass on the table. I poured about an eighth of an ounce. Brody took the bottle out of my hand.

"You can't feel nothing like that," he said. He poured me a sizable amount in my glass. I took a couple of sips. Brody smiled.

"Trust me," he said. "You'll forget about a lot of things with just a few more shots."

Brody seemed to get a thrill out of watching me turn the bottle up. He sat there until I had emptied my glass, and without hesitation, poured me another glassful.

The music in the juke box turned to a song about love. The more I listen, the more I drank. I started to feel warm and fuzzy inside. I turned the bottle up this time, and down the rest. I didn't want any sober time to think about myself or anyone else. My comfort was the thought of getting a good shot of Jack Daniel's and being left alone.

The song ended. I dragged over to the jukebox and found "Only the Strong Survive." I listened to the lyrics, this time, taking every word in like medicine.

Boy, boy, boy walking 'round with your head hung down.
I wouldn't let the little girl know that she made you feel like a clown.
There's going to be a whole lot of trouble in life, so get up off your knees,
cause only the strong survive . . . you better be strong, you better hold on."

Troubling thoughts returned. Why don't you end it all? What's the use of living? I struggled trying to keep those thoughts from taking over. I buried my head in my hands. The voice got louder and louder. I couldn't shut it out. You fool! What's there to live for?

I entertained the voice. What was there to live for? Everybody was gone. Over half of my platoon died along with my lieutenant and my buddies, Connelly and Billy. Besides that, even though I didn't know if Big Daddy had lived, I didn't have a clue to his condition.

And now, there was no hope of regaining the only woman I'd ever loved. She'd left a hole in my heart bigger than the Hoover Dam. I should have died with my men, I told myself. It was hard to control the part of my brain that kept urging me strongly to end it all—right then, right there.

I strategized how I would do it. I could get careless in the field with my rifle, start running until I crossed enemy lines, or I could drink myself to death. That sounded like a better idea. I didn't want a lot of pain. I wanted to slip away in the night.

It might have been the liquor that caused vivid images to come to mind. I'm not sure. But I had a flashback from as far back as the first day I arrived in the country. One of my comrades had run up to me after a mission.

"Did you hear what happened to Lieutenant Conway?" he asked, as he hung his head.

"No . . . what?" I asked.

"He got his head chopped off by the freaking chopper blades!" he said.

He told me that one of our lieutenants was walking to the LOH, a small chopper. Lieutenant Conway was about 6 feet 7 inches tall, and he forgot to duck. Before anyone could warn him, the blades cut his head off.

I took another deep swallow of my liquor. I thought about everything that had gone wrong since I'd been in the war, and there was no relief in sight.

I had arrived at the club around eleven o'clock that morning, and I left at midnight. I drank about a dozen beers and more shots of whiskey than I could count before I passed out.

When I woke up the next morning, my head was hanging off my cot. I was disappointed I was still alive. They told me three men had to drag me back to my hooch. I don't know what happened to Brody, but I was certain he didn't leave until he saw I was wasted.

I looked over at the empty cots of Connelly and Billy. Pictures of their families and friends were posted above their beds. The ribbons from gift packages were left next to Billy's music box where he'd place them. I couldn't remove anything from their beds like they'd asked me. I couldn't take the portraits down nor pack anything for them that day. I didn't know if I could ever do it for that matter.

I wanted more to drink, but I couldn't pull myself up to go back to the club.

The following day fresh turtles walked into base camp. One tall black guy introduced himself as Jonas Gaines. I tried to smile and give him a warm welcome, but I couldn't help thinking how I wished we didn't have replacements. I didn't feel up to training the newcomers or getting them acclimated to the area. They served only as reminders of what happened in the Triangle.

Jonas was assigned to my hooch. He was talkative, the one thing I hated most about new replacements. They had no clue what we were experiencing, and the last thing I wanted was to be bombarded with questions.

Another new arrival followed behind Jonas. He was a young, white guy with red-hair and a few freckles on his nose. During the introductions, he said he was eighteen although he looked much younger. He said his name was Nate, and he was from a small town in Texas. In a way, he reminded me of Billy, though there was no physical resemblance. It was only his inquisitive nature that made me think of Billy.

I was getting better about my feelings toward whites, but I didn't know if Nate was bringing the same prejudice beliefs like the ones Connelly and Billy had when they arrived. If so, I wasn't up for the challenge. Honestly, I didn't want to become friends with blacks or whites. I was done with getting close to soldiers only to look at empty cots.

Immediately after the introductions, they loaded me with questions as I'd expected. What a terrible time they chose to talk about the war, and it was twice as bad to answer questions about what happened in the Triangle. I didn't want to alarm them about the war, so I showed them around the camp, introduced them to the other men that survived the ambush and headed to the NCO.

The club was full as usual. A movie was playing, and I thought I'd watch it. But I never got around to it after I got to the bar. After several drinks, I didn't know I was in the world.

I drank until I passed out, again. But, that didn't stop the nightmares. They were always about the enemy upon me with a knife to my throat or a gun at my head. If I could have slept standing straight up like a guard at Buckingham Palace, I would have. Routinely, I slept lying on my back, and sometimes I couldn't move. It felt like someone had me pinned down. I struggled desperately to wake up. The pressure would lift and I'd jump up, searching for the enemy. Sometimes, I'd dream only about Ava. I would be in a fight with bombs blasting all around me. Out of nowhere, the ghost of Ava would appear through the thick smoke. When I tried to reach her, she'd disappear. I hated when I had nightmares of Ava, because it left me feeling sick all over.

Morning came. My recollection was blurred. I hated Brody for starting me on liquor and whiskey, but I loved him for it, too. I didn't want to think about or feel anything. The longer I stayed drunk, the better.

All I could recall was staggering to the jukebox a couple of times and playing a song entitled, "War." Our transmitters were able to pick up music from America and songs were heard all over the country of Vietnam.

Jonas and Nate fit in quite nicely. Surprisingly, coming from the South and the same states of Connelly and Billy, Nate didn't know racial prejudice like they did. If so, he never voiced or showed it. It was most beneficial to me. I couldn't imagine going through the same thing with him as I did with Connelly and Billy.

Jonas and Nate fooled around with the other men all night long. They were talking to me, but I kept losing them in the conversation. I asked Jonas several times to repeat everything he'd said to me.

"I know your mind's not here, man." Jonas said. You want to talk about it?"

"No, not really," I said.

"Well, when you're ready, I'm all ears," he said.

We sat across from a couple of men rolling weed. I watched to see if Jonas was going to join them, but he didn't.

It was a good two weeks later before I felt like socializing with the men. Up until then, I'd answer a question and that was it. When anyone tried to talk with me, I'd give them a look to leave me alone.

One day, I struck up a conversation with Nate while he was sitting with some other men that were getting to know him. He was quite amusing. If I could describe his features, it would be much like Gomer Pyle from the Andy Griffin Show. When he talked, even his mouth twisted like Gomer's. His mannerism and tone of voice was the epitome of the TV actor. He was medium in height with a close-to-the scalp haircut that displayed a visible small brown spot, about the size of a penny in the top. I asked him about it, and he said that it was his birth mark.

He started talking about how he spent his time at home on the weekends. We couldn't believe it. All he did was drive around his parent's ranch. Occasionally, he would hang out at the downtown diner. I thought he was joking at first, but I found out he was serious.

Later on, the guys started talking about the war. A deep frown formed in Nate's forehead. "Just what are we fighting for, anyway?" he asked.

We all exchanged looks. It was a question that had been in our discussions many times. One man laughed and said, "If you don't know, we sure as hell can't tell ya!"

There was a raucous of laughter. The men teased Nate for awhile about his naïve thinking and his quiet southern living, but he didn't seem to mind. In fact, he found more amusing stories to tell about his upbringing that made some guys tumble over with laughter.

I understood Nate. Having been born in a small town in the southern part of the mountains of North Carolina, there was not much excitement going on. There was almost no crime except for young boys stealing hubcaps or getting cut at the club, usually over some girl. Neighbors were always watching out for you. Everybody got along, or it seemed so.

I wasn't trying to make friends with Nate, but the more he talked, the more I liked him. When asked if he had a girlfriend, he laughed and said, "Can't say I have. Never been with one in my life."

One man smiled, jokingly. "By the time you come back from the village, you'll be a changed man." He leaned into Nate's face. "For the better, my friend."

The guys teased Nate a lot more. He took it all in strides.

Jonas joined our conversation. I found out he was married. We spent a lot of time talking about his wife and family. It was refreshing to talk about subjects other than our next mission.

As I listened to Jonas, I became somewhat envious of his close relationship with his wife. He talked on and on about his wife. They had a couple of children. He then asked the question I dreaded.

"What about you? Do you have a wife or girlfriend?"

"Apparently, I haven't met the right one to have my houseful of kids," I answered.

Jonas chuckled. "Oh? How many do you plan on having?"

"Maybe ten or more," I said.

"No wonder they run from you," Jonas said, laughing.

I struggled trying to stay in the conversation as I constantly fought images of Jerome and Ava wrapped in the arms of each other.

"So, have you ever been serious about a woman?" Jonas asked.

"One time," I answered.

"What happened?" he asked.

"Wrong time, wrong woman, I guess," I said.

I wanted him to end the conversation. I supposed he got the message that I didn't want to talk about it, because he dropped the subject.

I enjoyed talking with Jonas, but I was reluctant to get too close to him. For the most part, I didn't want to get close to him or Nate. I couldn't afford another tight brotherhood like I had with Connelly and Billy for fear they, too, would be killed.

Nate was naïve, much like I was when I arrived in South Nam. Coming from such a sheltered life, he'd never had a drink of alcohol or smoked a cigarette. Guys played on his innocence, particularly on the fact he'd never been with a woman. He had no street sense whatsoever. They told him things, and he believed every word.

One day, as we traveled into the village to the massage parlor,Nate and I walked side by side along the man-made trail.

"Listen, here," I said. "Don't mind these men who are edging you on to get a woman. It's your first and you've got to be careful."

"I'm not stupid, you know," Nate said, his voice rising.

I stopped in front of him, placing both hands on his shoulders. The other men passed us, shaking their heads and snickering.

"I know you aren't stupid," I said, calmly. "But these village women can get attached to you really quick. And before you know it, you will want to see them more and more. You've got to stay focused."

I felt like a hypocrite telling him to stay focused when that was the last thing I'd done since I'd been in the war. Nate was much like me when I fell in love, green behind the ears.

"I don't want you to make my mistake . . . falling for someone who won't take your love and affection seriously," I said.

Nate listened, but I wasn't sure he got all of what I was trying to say. However, it didn't stop me from telling him the truth as I saw it. He was profoundly confident that he knew what love and romance was all about, but he didn't have a clue. I wasn't an expert on love, but I was well acquainted with the grief and the emotional devastations caused by a failed relationship.

Back in my hooch, I reached for a bottle of whiskey I had placed under my mattress. I filled my gut with the warm, soothing liquor and then put some in my canteen.

If I went more than a few hours, I had to have a drink. As soon as I had finished one bottle, I was looking for another. It was an odd thing, though. I never felt the alcohol when I was in the field. I was keenly aware of my surroundings and enemy attacks. I never staggered. I stayed ready and alert to fulfill my oath—search, kill, and destroy.

I pulled out my Bible to the place where I'd placed Ava's picture. I didn't intend on reading the Bible, but my eyes caught a passage.

Set me as a seal upon your heart, as a seal upon your arm;
for love is strong as death and jealousy is cruel as the grave.

Its flashes are flashes of fire, a most vehement flame.
Many waters cannot quench love, neither floods drown it.

I stopped on the last line. "Many waters cannot quench love, neither floods drown it." It was the absolute truth of what I was experiencing. Perhaps, if I'd thought to read the bible, I would have avoided falling in love altogether. I'd known the power of love—that the levies of my heart were not strong enough to hold back its force. Love had me in its grip and wouldn't let go, occupying every inch of my being. It hurt to hold on, but it hurt even more to let go.

CHAPTER 14

We had one more week at base camp. Then we'd prepare for another mission in Tru Duc. I got nervous at the thought of returning to the jungle. The ambush in the Triangle hunted me day and night. For weeks, I had the stench in my nostrils of fresh, warm blood. I could still see my fallen comrades' flesh particles in my clothing. As much as I tried, I couldn't get their voices or their feeble cries out of my head.

The men started talking about the monsoon. That time of the year, the missions ahead were dreaded ones. Several men told us about the amount of rain to expect. That much water, I thought, was bound to make conditions almost unbearable for fighting. The morning of our mission, I asked my CO about it.

"It's like someone loading a barrel of water and dumping it on you every half an hour," he said. "You dry out one minute and before you know it, you're drenched again."

"All of us smell like stinking horse shit when we dry out." He chuckled as he went on. "The worst is yet to come. It's hard as hell trying to fight when it starts."

It didn't matter much to me whether there were drenching rain or blazing hot rays from the sun, I'd already experienced so much hell that it made no difference to me. I spent a lot of time smoking and drinking. Brody saw to that. The more alcohol I consumed, the more I wanted it. But if I'd known the consequences that night of my excessive consumption of alcohol, I would've thought twice about turning up the bottle that day.

We'd just arrived in Tru Duc and begun setting up our NPD.

Jonas exchanged places with me and took my round of watch duty. Nate and the rest of the men in my squad settled down to rest.

Out of the blue, Jonas started talking about a girl back home who was a good friend of his wife's.

"Her name's Trina," he said. "She has been friends with us for a long time. She's good people, and easy to talk with."

It took me by surprise that he brought up her name, and I wasn't sure of his motive. I brushed it off.

"That's good," I said. I reached for my canteen of liquor. Before I could take a sip, I felt dizzy. I didn't know whether it was the heat getting the best of me, or if it was the alcohol I'd loaded on before we left base. Moments later, I was engulfed with blackness. I lifted my hands in front of my face.

"Hey, Jonas. . . I can't see!" I said.

"Yeah, right," he said, with a chuckle.

"No . . . I'm not kidding. I can't see!" I said, as I stood up.

Nate shook me.

"C'mon, man," he said. "Stop fooling."

Another soldier shouted. "He's just stoned. You know what's in his canteen. Jack Daniel's his woman."

They all laughed.

I fanned my hands in front of me, trying to touch someone.

"Somebody help me. I'm telling you, I can't see," I yelled.

My heart was racing madly. I thought it would burst through my chest any moment. Suddenly, the laughter stopped.

"I think he's serious," Nate said. I felt him in front of me.

"Can you see my hands?" he asked.

"What? See what?" I urged.

"He needs a medic. He's not joking," I heard Jonas say.

I felt hands on my back and arms as they got me to sit down. By the time a medic got to me, I was sweating profusely. I kept moving my hands in front of my face hoping for a glimpse of something—anything. Nothing was moving, at least, not that I could see. The darkness seemed blacker than a hundred midnights. I broke into chills.

A couple of men left their post and helped the medic get me out of the area. I felt guilty for putting my men at a terrible risk in the battle zone. We needed every man in my squad on that mission.

Fearful thoughts raced through my head. Would I ever see the faces of my family, again? Had I seen the last of the green grass and trees, the blue skies, and the rocky roads of Lenoir? What if I have to be confined to bed?

I don't know where they took me, but I felt isolated from everyone. I presumed I was at our base camp hospital when I heard two doctors speaking about my condition. Their medical words were far beyond me.

"Can you tell me what's going on?" I asked, desperately.

"We're running a few tests, soldier," one doctor replied. He and the other physician stepped away from my bed. I heard them speaking in low voices not too far from me. I heard them say, "He's been drinking that gook whiskey."

I wasn't sure what else was said, but I knew the news wasn't going to be good. I felt faint and disoriented at intervals.

Ava's face appeared clearly to me in the darkness. Then, like the nightmares, she faded away slowly. I was clouded in darkness—both kinds. I couldn't see my way out of the despair of losing her, nor could I see how to find my own shoes. It felt like I was in a deep pit.

"We're going to run some tests, soldier," I heard a physician say. Afterwards, there was no more movement around me for a long time. I drifted off to sleep.

After a couple of days, I got my lab results. The medics told me alcohol had damaged the nerves in my body. I had a mixture of formaldehyde and carbolic acid along with several other poison agents that had infected my body. The Vietnamese called the whiskey, "Boom de Boom".I was to undergo treatment, the doctor said, and that would determine the overall outcome. He told me only six cases of this condition had ever been reported in Vietnam. Unfortunately, I was one of them.

"Will I see again?" I asked.

"I suspect you will," he answered. "You could have died." He paused and took a deep breath. "Let me put it this way, you should be dead. Your body is highly contaminated. Right now, it's a matter of time. In a few days, we will know how much damage was done to your system."

I listened while pondering. If that much poison was in my body, then why wasn't I dead? I was alive and I still didn't understand why.

Each day, my vision got better. Then, after three days, I had regained my sight. It felt great returning to my unit and seeing my comrades. However, despite my blessed recovery and the jubilant soldiers' cheers, sadness overwhelmed me.

The men patted me on my back and pulled me out of my hooch, leading me into the NCO club to celebrate. They say fools never learn. I guess I was the biggest one that had ever been born. As soon as I got inside, I grabbed a seat at the bar and ordered a shot of whiskey.

The "Bring the Boys Home" song wasn't playing. For awhile, it rang out all over the country. Some guys were reported as going AWOL because of this anti-war song. After a few weeks, our CO told us that the American Armed Force banned the song and that it could not be played anymore. It was just as well, because for the first time, I didn't want to hear it. It only made me nostalgic for home. After the Iron

Triangle, I wanted nothing more than to see the small mountain town with its aged buildings, the corner grocery store, and the road leading to my house. I wanted to hear the sounds of my sisters and brothers fussing over the TV channels, to see smoke coming from the chimney on a cold winter day, and to smell country ham frying on my mother's stove. I envied the men who'd be getting out in a few weeks and would be on their way to the good, old USA.

I stayed at base for a few days and spent all of my time at the bar in the club. I kept beckoning the bartender for more whiskey, and he kept refilling my shot glass. I turned up the glass, and before I could swallow, I felt a light tap on my shoulder.

"You've had enough," Jonas said. "You gotta lay off that stuff. Why don't you come with us to the village tomorrow and let them gals give you a good work over?

I shook my head. "No. I'm through with women."

"So, you're crossing over to the other side?" he asked, laughing.

"No," I said, emphatically. "A man can't do nothing for me. Besides, it's nothing wrong with wanting to be alone, is there? Females are trouble. I don't need them right now."

Some guys overheard our conversation and burst into laughter.

"You're as good as dead if you don't want a woman," one man said. "And I don't see any real man out here that can say I'm wrong."

"The only thing left for you is the priesthood," another guy bellowed.

I ignored all of them and turned back to my whiskey. Jonas pushed the shot glass from me, and I politely reached for it and pulled it back.

"It numbs me," I said.

Another slow, sad song came on the reel-to-reel. I thought about Ava and closed my eyes. Maybe, just maybe, it's all a dream. I thought to myself. And, one day, I'd wake with her in my arms once more.

Jonas saw that he couldn't convince me to lay off the bottle, so he finally left, leaving me to my own fate. Before long, I put my head on the bar and blacked out.

I'd drunk so much that night I ended up in the hospital, again, for observation. They said I'd drunk two six packs of beer and a fifth of liquor. I didn't doubt it. I lost count after my sixth Bud.

I never thought about the destructive effects of the cool liquid sliding down my throat and soothing my body. All I wanted to do was rid myself of the hurt and pain from Ava's letter. She spoke as though what we had was nothing more than a fling.

I'm not sure who got me to the hospital, but I woke up on a bed in a corner of the room. A nurse approached my side.

"You had quite a night last night," she said, as she placed a thermometer in my mouth. I grunted from the throbbing pain in my head.

She removed the thermometer and read it. "It's 101."

"What was it before?" I asked.

"Oh, dear . . . you were in bad shape earlier," she said with a frown. "It was very high, 105 and climbing. That's not good." She felt my arm. "And you were cold."

She looked at me with a serious stare.

"Do you think you need to see a doctor to talk with you about your problems?" she asked.

I frowned at her. I was like any other soldier, I thought. We all smoked and drank. Of course, I might have drunk more liquor than the average soldier, but I wasn't mentally unstable.

"What problems?" I asked, staring back at her.

"Well, from your charts, you have a serious drinking problem and . . ."

Frustrated, I stared at her. "I don't need a shrink if that's what you're suggesting."

"I'm only saying that sometimes you might need someone to listen to you," she said. "Any more alcohol and it would have been shooting through your pores."

"I'm all right," I said. "Drinking helps me forget."

She placed her small fingers on top of mine.

"Let someone in," she said. "Talk to somebody. Getting a psychiatrist to see you isn't a shame. It doesn't mean you're crazy, mad or anything of that sort. We all need a friend."

She patted my hand and walked off. She reminded me of my mother with her soft voice and gentle touch. I knew she meant well by suggesting psychiatric care. But for a second, I was irritated about her suggestion. She spoke as though she knew talking with a doctor would cure all of my problems. My condition might have looked to her like a quick fix, but that was far from reality. She never asked me about what drove me to my heavy drinking. I don't think she cared. If I'd told her about me and Ava—that I trusted a woman with my heart and soul, and she killed me a million times over with her venomous words, would it have made a difference? I resented anyone telling me what they thought I needed. I was grappling with whether to live or die. The idea of letting a mere stranger sit and asked questions so he could get inside my head was laughable.

I turned over that night and studied the cots with men stretched out. I wondered how they were coping. Had they given up? What shrink could get them straightened out when they discovered their lower extremities had been removed?

Late that evening, Jonas walked in. With a hearty smile, he shook my bed.

"Hey, wake up," he said. "How are you feeling?"

"Lousy," I answered, taking a puff off a fresh lit Marlboro. "What are you doing here? I thought you'd be at the club."

"Had to come see about my friend," he said. "What's the doc saying?" He reached for my pack of cigarettes.

"That if I come back in here, they will finish me off themselves," I said. "They think I don't want to live."

Jonas dragged a metal chair to my bed and straddled it. "If this war don't get you, that bottle sure will," he said, as he flicked a light to his tobacco.

"Everybody's telling me to lay off the bottle," I said. "But they don't understand. It's the only thing that gives me relief."

"It wears off, and then what?" Jonas said. "You still got the problem. You're drinking enough for four men."

He leaned into me. "Wanna talk about it . . . or her?"

"How do you know it's a woman?"

"I don't know," he said. "I only know somebody saw you messed up the other day with a letter in your hand. Men talk."

I thought about Brody who was in my hooch when I got Ava's letter. He must have told Jonas about the bad shape I was in.

Jonas leaned into me. "What happened?"

He took a deep draw of his cigarette and waited for my response. Up until then, I hadn't talked about Ava. Connelly and Billy were the only men I had spoken with about her. But even then, I was careful not to tell them everything that had happened between us.

"I don't want to waste your time," I said.

"Don't you think I need to be the judge of that?" Jonas asked. "I might have the cure for your ailment. I can read your mind."

"So, you're some kind of psychic?" I asked, laughing.

"No, not really," he said. "I went through too much hell not to know when a man's head is messed up over a woman.

He tossed the empty Marlboro pack in a corner.

"You see, my wife and I haven't always been together," he said. "I mean, we split for about six months. I guess it was partly my fault, because I was never home. My job kept me on the go."

He took another draw, exhaled and sent smoke spiraling upward and away from me.

"The funny thing," he said. "I didn't know she was miserable. She was a quiet person, never said anything unless she it was that time of the month, you know?" He laughed out loud. "Then she had complaints about everything."

"How did you find out she was unhappy?" I asked.

"I came home one day and her things were gone," he said. "She moved in with a friend. Finally, we met at a restaurant and she told me everything about our marriage that was wrong. Then she heard the way I felt. There are some things, still, that we're working on. So, you see, you're not alone."

He leaned back in his seat, and he looked at me with concern.

"So, female troubles, eh?"

I nodded.

"Well, I think I got just the cure for you," he said.

"And what's that?" I asked.

"A gal back home," he said.

I almost choked and sprang up. I stared him straight in the face.

"Maybe it's you who needs a shrink," I said.

With an urgent plea in his voice, he said. "Now hear me out before you say that. I've been thinking about it a lot. She's a nice girl and fits your speed."

I put up my hand in front of his face.

"Hold up. I'm not interested," I said. "I don't think you know how much a female has complicated my life in the past few months.

"Maybe so," he said. "But there's a woman back home that is smart and witty . . . not to speak of her beauty."

Jonas wasn't letting up, but he pointedly carried on. "All I'm asking is that you let her write you, and if it's not what you want, then you haven't lost anything."

"No," I said, emphatically.

He kept on as though he didn't hear me. "She loves to have fun but can be serious all at the same time."

Jonas jokingly chewed his jaw, pretending he had a mouth full of food.

"And, she can cook," he carried on. "She could turn that tough buffalo into a mouth-watering, tender rib-eye that'd make you crow like a rooster!"

"Look, for the last time, the answer is negative," I said. "You're crazy, man."

"So, what do you think?" he asked, still ignoring my statements.

I reclined on my pillow with mixed emotions about the whole thing. A part of me wanted to start over, but it felt too strange. I thought about the dreadful task of learning someone new. Starting over meant letting my guard down, knowing who to trust, what to say, and making sure we both wanted the same thing. It was risky and full of uncertainties. On the other hand, I wanted so desperately to heal my broken heart, and the only way to do that was to come out of my cocoon and start trusting.

Jonas's gaze held steady. He kept watching me until I took in a deep breath and gave him what he wanted to hear.

"Whatever you do, I'm not making any promises," I said. "No one's ever going to hurt me, again."

"Sweet Jesus!" he said. "That's what I want to hear."

He tossed his chair to the side and squeezed my shoulder. Her name is Trina Wooden. You can thank me later."

I turned my back while he strolled away, whistling.

After he left, I was back to the old familiar—thinking about Ava. I tried to blot her face out of my head, but I couldn't. I was flooded with memories of her more than ever after Jonas left.

While I was in recovery, I had nightmares about the Triangle. Clear images of Connelly and Billy appeared as their lifeless bodies covered the ground where I should have been. I still couldn't get it in my head that I came out without them. Pondering the attack, my mother's words came back to me, "You will be wounded, but you won't die." Her prophesies were right so far. But I couldn't get too comfortable as if I'd cheated death. I had four more months in the country, a lot of time to get killed.

The next day I returned to base. Jonas joined me for drinks at the club. He talked a lot that day and shared some more of his life stories. The more intimate details he gave me about his marriage, the more relaxed I became around him. He was the first and only man who could engage me in a conversation and hold my attention.

I didn't plan to talk to him as much as I did about my life, but he had a way of pulling things out. I'd danced around sharing my Ava story until finally I decided it was time I let it all out. Before I knew it, I'd told him about what had happened and how I waited with hopes of her coming back to me. But instead, her letter was an obituary.

"I am haunted by her night and day," I said. "Every time I go into the village; the women remind me of her. They are her height, size, and shape. I can't stand to smell their sweet perfume or touch the softness of their skin."

Jonas was listening. I felt it was safe to go on—that I wasn't being judged for holding on to a ghost.

"I saw a Vietnamese woman toss her hair from her face," I said. "It reminded me of how Ava used to make the same gesture when her thick curls got in her way. Even the laughter of any woman sounds too much like her. I made love to the one of the most beautiful Vietnamese women, and I still feel lonely and empty. I tell you, I am plagued by Ava's spirit every minute of the day."

Mentioning her name made me pushed back tears. I paused several times to keep my voice from breaking.

"Maybe, I loved her too much," I said. "I didn't know love was supposed to hurt."

"It hurts like hell," Jonas said. "I've been there."

"With your wife?" I asked.

"No, with another woman before I met my wife," he said. "That's another story and not enough months in a year to tell you about it."

Jonas sat back as if in deep thought. There was long silence between us. His face swelled with compassion.

"I don't know all that you feel," he said. "But there's one thing I do know. You've gotta get out of this slump someway, somehow."

I knew he was right. But it was easy for him to say it. He wasn't me. I was the one who'd lost everything I'd ever loved or wanted, and there was nothing anyone could do to restore that and make me feel better.

We sat for several hours that night, talking about our personal experiences. We had more in common than differences when it came to women—some good experiences, some bad ones.

Jonas was a good listener. After that talk, I felt I could trust him. I couldn't remain in isolation. I was weary of holding onto the pain and the guilt. He was right. I had to let go of Ava. But the fact remained, I didn't know how.

About a month later, I had been in the field for a few weeks and returned to our base in Lai Khê. I had just put my gear down and started to unwind when Jonas came up to me. He was grinning from ear to ear.

"I told my wife about you . . . that you wanted Trina to write you," he said.

I was surprised he'd written home and told his wife about our conversation. Instantly, I got nervous about the idea of receiving mail from another woman. I felt vulnerable.

"I don't know, man" I said. "I didn't know you were really going to do this."

He patted me on the back.

"You'll be fine," he said. "And if you don't, I will bear the consequences for you."

CHAPTER 15

In about mid February, I received a box of canned food and a card from my mother, wishing me a happy birthday. My mouth flew open in shock. Not about my mother's package, but I looked at my small calendar and realized I'd missed my own birthday by four days. It was easy to lose track of time in the war. It had been ten months since I arrived in the South Vietnam, and February 22nd was like another day.

My mother made all birthdays special in our home, and even though I was thousands of miles away, it made no difference.

I pulled out packs of cookies and plenty of canned meats. Vienna sausage was amongst them. I reached down deep and discovered saltine crackers. Then I choked back tears when I saw the jar of Jiffy. My mother knew how fond I was of peanut butter. It was the little things that meant so much to us soldiers that people didn't get. My mother got it.

Several anxious men huddled over me as I plowed through the minuscule box as if they were expecting something inside with their names on it. I took my can opener and opened a can of pork in beans. Instantly, three spoons dug it. The guys thanked me, but I had no intentions of sharing as much as they took.

At base camp in Lai Khê, there was rumor my squad might have to go back into the Triangle. The mention of returning to the Triangle sent cold chills through me.

I overheard two men talking.

"If we gotta return to that hell, I'll shoot myself in the foot," one of them said. "We can do each other a favor. You with me?"

The other guy nodded.

I didn't really think that any soldier would contemplate harming himself. However, these two men sounded quite adamant. Their plans were to shoot each other, hoping to get a medical discharge from the war. Just like me, they were petrified about going back to that part of the jungle. I could hear it in their voices.

I quickly asked around to find out if the rumor was true.

"No," our sergeant said. "I haven't been given any orders for your men to go back there. Your squad is going back to the bush in a few days around Ben Cat, but there's no word about the Triangle. Don't get anxious until you hear from me."

It was the most blessed thing I'd heard that day. I went over to my hooch and informed some of my men of what I was told.

"Negative," I said to a couple of men. "We are not going there."

When they saw the smile on my face, they explored with cheers.

"Instead of orders to return to the Triangle," I said. "We'll be leaving for another mission in Ben Cat or some other place."

That kind of good news was worth celebrating. It spread throughout our squad, and we all headed to the club. The men ordered beers and started pouring liquor down each other's throat. At the same time, they were pulling the few women, who'd come to base camp, into separate corners.

One soldier danced wildly to the jukebox music, gathering empty beer cans and stomping them underneath his feet. It was a crazy party. I found a corner with a beer and watched the excitement. I laughed even when nothing was funny.

A couple of weeks passed and we were in Ben Cat. We plowed our way through the hot, massive jungle of weeds to guard a bridge. There were no safe missions, but this one wasn't considered as dangerous as the Triangle, our sergeant told us. Enemy contact would be minimal, he'd said. However, that was not to say they were taking a vacation. We huddled in rice patties as we waited for movement.

My back ached and my eyes burned, fiercely from lack of sleep. I was beyond exhaustion. Brody saw my hands trembling as I fumbled for my canteen. He handed me a small pouch.

"This will help calm you," he said.

Unlike other times, I decided to take Brody up on his offer. When I opened the pouch, two tiny pills were inside. I pulled my canteen of whiskey and with a quick swallow flushed one of the white tablets down and then the other.

I looked up and saw Jonas coming over to my dugout. He dropped down beside me and licked the bottom of his lips.

"Give me a swallow," he said. "My throat feels like a razor." I handed him my canteen. He took a sip.

"Damn, man!" he said, spitting a mouthful of whiskey onto the ground. "I can't believe you brought this shit with you."

A soldier next to Jonas placed his figure over his lips to quiet him. Jonas leaned into me and whispered.

"You're a damn fool," he said. "Do you know that?"

"It's my only friend," I said.

"It's your death ticket," he scolded.

The pills Brody gave me took an effect I wasn't expecting. I saw trees that looked like the enemy in rank walking toward me. They moved in stride with determination. I jumped to my feet and fired my rifle wildly. It seemed like hundreds of them were moving toward us.

"They're coming on us!" I said.

Someone yelled."He's on something. There's nothing out there!"

Jonas lunged for me and knocked me down, pulling me into some bushes. My CO and several other men came running over. After a couple of minutes, they got me settled. Soon after, I heard my CO cursing and swearing.

"Get him off this damn post!" he said. "He's not capable of being out here. I'll talk to him in the morning."

It didn't matter what he said or did, I was in no condition to care. At the moment, I didn't care about living or dying. It was all the same to me.

The next morning, I suffered from another severe headache. I was having them frequently, but this one was so violent that it made me shudder. I grunted like a wounded animal, tossing from side to side on my cot. Jonas came over to me.

"What in the hell got into you?" he asked, demandingly. "You looked like a crazy coyote."

"Brody gave me something to calm me," I said.

"That bastard!" Jonas said. He jumped up and rushed out of my hooch. I didn't have to ask, but I knew he was going to find Brody. I didn't care what Jonas would do or say. All I wanted was another drink of liquor and Tylenol.

The following day, I felt better. A bunch of the men wanted to go into the village. I decided to go with them.

I'd been drinking as usual. When I walked inside the club, I saw a young soldier engaged in a heated conversation with a sergeant. He was an older man, perhaps in his early forties. I didn't like the tone the soldier was using toward the sergeant. In an effort to catch what they were arguing about, I worked my way over.

By the sound of it, the soldier was angry with something the sergeant did to him some time ago. It was apparent the sergeant was not going to stand for such verbal abuse. He stood in front of the soldier with his shoulders squared. His stance was straight. His countenance was bold and daring. The soldier continued his argument. His voice escalated. By this time, everyone in the village club had heard them arguing. I watched the interaction closely. The soldier's liquor had gotten to him. More words were exchanged. In one quick motion, the soldier gave the sergeant a big push, causing the sergeant to fall to the floor. The old sergeant looked feeble against the youth's vigor. It wasn't my fight, but I had a flashback of grade school when I was bullied.

Before I knew it, I'd lunged for the soldier. I pulled him off the sergeant and threw him against the wall.

"Let me go!" the soldier yelled as I pressed him against the wall with my hand on his throat. His breathing was labored.

"Are you stupid?" I yelled, through clenched teeth. "You've just assaulted a master sergeant!" I probably wouldn't have responded so violently if I hadn't been drinking. But the soldier needed to be taught a lesson, I thought. And with my pent up frustrations, it felt good to rough up somebody.

The soldier struggled to break away as I tightened my grip around his neck. In only a few seconds, I felt hands on my shoulders. With a strong thrust forward, two soldiers rushed me out of the club. The soldier staggered off as someone helped the sergeant off the floor.

I was taken straight to the headquarters for questioning. Unfortunately, my reasoning for breaking up the fight was not enough for the ranking officials. I sat calmly in the small room at headquarters to hear my fate.

"That was not your fight," a lieutenant said.

"With all due respect, sir," I said. "I was doing what most cowards in the room did not do . . . defend a sergeant."

"Interference is what we call it," he said. "When a soldier is in conflict with an officer, that officer is more than capable of defending himself."

"I beg to differ, sir," I said.

"How so?" he asked.

This time he moved a stack of papers over and sat on the edge of the desk.

"The sergeant was too old", I said. "His physical strength didn't match that soldier's."

"Nevertheless, it wasn't your fight," he said.

"And this war isn't, either," I said. I could feel the heat rising on the back of my neck.

"Am I detecting a disposition contrary to a sworn duty?"

"I was sworn to duty by others' decisions, not mine," I said. "None of us in that room volunteered for this war. We were drafted in the name of 'humanitarian', for a country we don't live in or know anything about."

I listened to my own voice and was surprised I was saying things I wanted to say from the day I arrived.

"In case you haven't noticed, I'm a black man. My race is dying in America in the fight for humanitarian. That war makes sense to me. This one does not."

He took a deep breath and returned to behind his desk. His looked agitated, and I didn't know what was coming next.

"You may leave," he said. "Understand, however, that I'm writing an Article 15."

I walked out and back to my hooch. I was written up for misconduct and ordered to stay away from the village club for awhile. It stunned me that I was penalized for my righteous act. Jonas felt the same.

"So let me get this right," Jonas said. "You were written up with an Article 15 because you saved the old the old man from getting beat up?"

I nodded.

Jonas laughed. "You should have let that guy beat the hell out of him."

The following day, I resorted back to my introversion. I avoided downtime with the men and wrote letters to my mother. The Article

15 was dismissed after my lieutenant looked at my good combat status while on missions.

That night on watch duty, I pulled out a picture of Ava and stared at it. The pain returned to me. No matter how hard I tried to fight my feelings for Ava, I realized I was still hopelessly in love. I couldn't destroy her pictures or letters. I stuffed the photo back into my bag and went back to my watch duty.

It was October, and the monsoon season had started. My squad had been ordered to fight near the An Loc river. I got my rucksack with bug repellent, ChapStick, and other items necessary for the mission and waited with my men for the chopper.

We experienced periods of sunshine followed by a heavy downpour, leaving us drenched. It was exactly like I'd been warned. The monsoon rains had no mercy on us. It was expected to continue for weeks. It had already washed away topsoil and created deep mud holes, making it difficult to walk, especially with aching feet and heels. My feet were constantly soaked. When I removed my boots, water blisters had formed on my toes and on the bottom of my feet. The smell was awful.

Thick thunderous clouds dropped barrels of water upon us. Each downpour grew heavier and heavier. It was not only difficult to walk or run, but there were times when we couldn't see twenty feet in front of us, and we were never dry for more than twenty minutes.

After a while, the wind picked up. It started as a low whistle and grew into a vociferous heavy hissing. The winds got stronger by the seconds. I tried to run for cover, but it was impossible to move against the force of wind. I held onto a tree stump with tangled roots and vines. In the distance, I heard my comrades yelling. I saw one man clinging to a bush. A soldier fell on top of him and held on. The storm turned more violently with heavy wind and rain. There were loud rumbles of thunder, and sharp lightning raced the sky. Strong wind gusts sent branches and debris flying into the air.

A loud crash from flying branches was heard nearby. I wasn't sure where all of my comrades had run for cover, but the yells stopped.

The force of wind almost lifted me into the sky. I clutched to the tree and prayed. I didn't see my life flash before my eyes like some people, but I knew I was at death's door. Suddenly, as if my body had been transcended into another space and time, I heard music like the violins of my mother's church and the gibberish language coming from a mass of people. I didn't know enough about the supernatural, but I was certainly experiencing an unusual phenomenal.

About ten minutes later, the wind and rain gradually ceased. I looked around for some form of life. Quietness had settled with moderate winds. A few seconds later, my comrades came into view.

"What in the hell was that?" one of them said.

"I don't know," I answered. "I'm just glad it's over."

We all were alive. By the looks and sounds of it all, we determined it was a typhoon, a storm common for that time of year—between July and November.

We hunted for our supplies. Most of them were tossed in all different directions. After we'd gathered what little we could savage, we headed to base.

That experience had a profound effect on me. Although I wasn't a saint of any kind, I believed in God. By now, I was convinced a higher power was keeping me alive for a reason far beyond my human ability to understand. I'd hoped one day it would become clear.

After I got back to base camp, our mail caught up with us. I got my first letter from Trina.

Dear Ken,

Jonas, my good friend, told me about you and that you might like to hear from someone new from the states. I'm living a single life and could use the company, myself. So, if you feel the urge, write me whenever you can.

Warmest, Trina

I read the letter and put it aside. It was good to hear from a female other than my mother, but I wasn't ecstatic. As with any letter I'd received, I tucked it into my duffel bag along with the others.

One night at base, after the monsoon season had stopped, I walked outside. There was clear sky overhead. I sat on top of a sack and gazed into the sky. The sparkling stars and the full moon had a calming effect on me. I studied the elements with Ava on my mind. The sky looked much like the night I scooped her up and took her to Lovers Cove and made love to her for the first time. I could see her eyes searching mind as she waited for my touch. Her soft laughter was in my ears; her smile fading as her lips met mine.

I sat there a few minutes with my private thoughts.

Jonas walked up.

"I didn't mean to snap at you so hard out there," he said. "But you don't need that stuff, particularly not in the bush, man. I had a talk with Brody. He'll never try that trick on you, again. Anyway, ten days and he's out of here."

That was good to know. I never thought Brody was doing nothing more but wanting someone to get high with him. He just happened to choose me.

"That crap could've killed you," Jonas said.

"I died a long time ago," I said. "Do you know how it feels to be thousands of miles away and get a letter from the only woman you've ever loved, saying she never want to see you again?"

Jonas turned to listen.

"I deserved better treatment," I went on. "Was it a habit she had to string a guy along and then drop him like a hot iron?"

"I don't know," Jonas said. "But you've got to pull yourself together and get on with your life.

"Well, to ease your mind, I got a letter from Trina," I said.

Jonas had started to leave, but he stopped in his tracks. He looked as if I'd given him tickets to the super bowl.

"That's great!" he said.

"It's not that easy to get involved," I said. "I don't know . . ."

"Just give her a chance," he said. "It can't hurt. It's the best thing you'll ever do. Trust me."

When Jonas left, I assessed my emotional state. I wanted to be loved by a woman. I needed the healing that maybe only a female could bring. I wanted desperately to get rid of Ava's ghost that stalked me day and night. I tried to hate her for hurting me, but even that seemed impossible. Each town or village we entered, there were plenty of women. We could get prostitutes at any time. They were there specifically for us GI's. But none of them could fulfill the desire for what was once my own.

I wanted to be free, but I held on to the memories of Ava like a heroin addict. I wasn't angry anymore. I was past that. But I missed her more than anything. I felt lonely. It hurt to think about her, and it hurt to stop. I was miserable when I closed my eyes, and I hated the light of day.

I didn't see Brody after that day in the bush. He didn't show up at my hooch. I figured he was somewhere preparing to leave. I never knew what Jonas said to him, and I never cared to find out.

A new lieutenant joined our rank. He walked in as we were gearing up to go on to our next mission. All of our new replacements were in.

I looked around the room. The new men looked anxious and ready to go, much like I was when I first arrived. I felt grief for them. They had no idea what was ahead or how much there was to learn about war.

We took turns pulling guard duty around the perimeter of the compound two hours on, two hours off. Every man looked extremely fatigued. Some of the men had to have their weed while on duty. They said marijuana was their way of coping. All I wanted was my canteen full of liquor.

About three weeks, the mail came. To my surprise, I got another letter from Trina. She wrote a longer one this time.

Dear Ken,

I have been sitting here at the bus stop thinking about you. It's such a pleasant day. No clouds at all. I'm on my way to the supermarket now, and then I'll take some food to this homeless man I met. I enjoy helping people. I can't wait to see you. I know you would like to taste some American food for a change (smile). I love to cook.

I pray for you often, for your safety and all.

Take care, Trina

I saw Jonas standing outside with a group of guys and called him over. I read the letter out loud. He laughed and said. "See, I told you she's perfect for you!"

"We'll see," I said. "I'm just not feeling it right now."

"Trust me," he said, grinning. "She's great. You will know what I'm talking 'bout when you see her."

After a few days, I started spending time with Cho Phi. The men in my camp teased me about her being my gal. She was gorgeous and delightful to be with, even though I knew there were other men in her life. But I had no feelings for her that way. This made it easy for me to see her.

"I am your girl," she said, one evening. Her eyes danced in her head when she spoke. I took what she said lightly at first until I looked in her eyes and saw she was serious. Big Daddy had warned me. "When a Vietnamese woman says you're her man, you better run for your damn life," he said. "She's gonna want you to take her home with you. Never let her know when you are leaving."

He had stuck a cigar in his mouth. Then he leaned into my ear. "And, if you don't take them, they'll never let you leave. They have a way of making you very uncomfortable," he chuckled a little.

His remark that day had made me uneasy. I couldn't imagine falling in love with Cho Phi and taking her to America, but I thought seriously about what Big Daddy's wisdom was telling me. I thought it might be best to leave her alone.

I never had to give her money like the other men. All I needed to do was buy her some Saigon tea. Her eyes brightened when she got it. It was a rich delicacy to the women, like Champaign or the finest wines in America.

When I got back to camp, the men were having fun with Nate, plotting to get a female for him. I walked in on their conversation while they made plans to take him into the village with them. Nate was all ears, hanging on every word. I pulled him aside.

"The worst thing you can do is to listen to these guys," I said, sternly. "These Vietnamese women will take your money and leave you. Trust me. From now on, you just listen to me."

Nate nodded dutifully, but I could see him thinking mighty hard.

A week passed and things had been quiet. I was sure something was going to happen, that we could expect an attack at any moment. My suspicion was accurate.

At base that night, while we were asleep, I heard a thumping sound a distance away. My ears were trained to that sound.

"Cover!" I called out.

No sooner than I'd alerted the men, we were hit with mortar fire. We dived behind whatever was near. We waited, but no more attacks came. It was only one blast, but Nate was balled over and shaking like a cold, wet kitten.

"Are you all right?" I asked.

He nodded.

"This is how it's going to be all the time," I said. "And you ain't never gonna get used to it. That's why you need to keep your mind off village women and on this war."

That was precisely the advice Big Daddy gave me when I first entered the country.

We were fortunate that no one was injured or killed. The rest of the night was spent watching and waiting.

Trina's letters kept pouring in. One day, Jonas came up to me and asked if I'd heard from her. I pulled out a recent letter from my pocket and handed it to him. Jonas couldn't stop grinning after he read the letter. He handed it back to me and put his hands in both pockets. Jonas then rocked back on his heels like an old farmer who'd just got his best harvest.

"You can thank me later," he said, with a satisfied look.

Each letter revealed more about her. She worked for a dentist in a small office downtown. Her favorite past-time was reading mystery novels. She enjoyed collecting coins and foreign stamps. The best part of all, she loved to cook. That sounded great to me.

I asked Jonas if he'd told Trina about me and Ava. He assured me that he hadn't mentioned a word about what happened to us.

"Trust me. Trina has written you without any personal info from me," he said.

I sat with there with a troubling thought. What if I opened my soul only to get another knife in my heart?

Later that evening, a soldier walked up to me. He told me there was a second rumor about my platoon returning to the Iron Triangle. Instantly, my insides started jumping.

"It can't be!" I said.

Later on, I found out that the soldier who kept starting these rumors was having mental problems. I was told he became extremely paranoid after his experience in the Triangle. I understood precisely how he felt. Nightmares of that ambush kept me on edge, too. I couldn't phantom the thought of returning to the Triangle. Each time we got orders, my blood rushed to my head and my knees weakened. The war was having an ill effect on all of us, and I wasn't sure what my own mental condition would be after it was over.

Finally, my platoon got orders for Ben Cat. It was wide-open territory outside of a village lined with a lot of rice patties. Although it was hot, a slight breeze would sweep occasionally across my face, cooling my forehead. We traveled a distance from the bridge in the blazing sun until we found a place to set our ambush.

We secured our position and settle down for our chop chop. There was no activity from the enemy that day, and we took full advantage of it. We had some time to eat and rest before moving on. Our C-rations consisted of canned beans, mixed sometimes. And if we were lucky, they were mixed with turkey, chicken, or beef. We heated our food with C-4, but we had to be careful. The can was highly active and could easily explode.

It was not unusual to run short on water, and we did. We followed our regular routine of drawing the contaminated water from our bomb craters, dropping a purifying tablet and washing down our food. It was business as usual.

We left our base, and we went into the village. It was full of pretty Vietnamese girls scouting about. The women were eager to see us and immediately offered their services. I cast my eyes at Nate. He was carefully scrutinizing each woman as we passed. One of our men slapped him on the back.

"Hey, my man." he said. "You got lots of choices. Don't be bashful."

Nate laughed along with the other men with him. He'd gotten use to their foolish jesting even though I was bothered by it. When the men found out that Nate didn't have a girlfriend, they cleverly devised a plan. One man pulled him off to the side and made the introductions to a couple of women. I walked over to Nate.

"Listen," I said. "You don't have to fall for what these guys are telling you. Remember what I told you."I watched him the entire time we were in the village for fear if he was left unguarded, he'd sleep with the first woman he saw. And then he would become attached to her.

Despite all of the advice I offered, Nate couldn't resist the suggestions of the men. That evening, some other men paid one of the Vietnamese girls to break him in. I knew it was a cold trick, but it seemed to work.

After his encounter with a girl in the village, Nate later returned with a big smile on his face. A couple of men saw him coming and stood to applaud him. They knew what'd happened and slapped him on the back.

When I learned Nate had given the woman almost all of his much money—about two hundred US dollars—I almost punched him. "That's it!" I said. "No more experimenting for you. You're gonna lose your mind out here."

The men laughed and continued interrogating him. They wanted to know the details about his first time with a woman, and what name he gave his new girl. Nate mumbled something and they roared with laughter.

I stood looking at Nate's excitement. Finally, I had to smile. As much as I hated to admit it, his first time made him more sociable. When he first arrived, he was quiet and shy. Now he was laughing, and his face glowed.

I watched as he caroused with the men while they talked about women. Suddenly, I was saddened for him. The next test the men would give him would be his first taste of whisky. I knew he wasn't ready for liquor no more than he was ready for the charming Vietnamese women. Even though he was in the army and was made to fight like a man, he had a lot to learn about life and women as we all did. Almost all of us were still in our late teens or early twenties, too stupid to tell a chicken from a goose.

I didn't feel right drinking while Nate was nearby, so I was careful not to let him see me getting drunk. Even though it was expected for every soldier to drink or smoke at some point, I wanted to set a good example for him. Looking at Nate was like looking at me in the mirror. I knew what the military life could do to a soldier—especially a soldier in combat.

"It's a lonely life away from the one you love and care about," I said to Nate later on. "No matter how much support a man gets from his comrades, it's not the same as having the one he loves care for him. So, you don't want to get messed up here, because this is not the real world back home."

Could I save Nate? Probably not. But I could warn him and be a friend.

Weeks passed, and another letter came from Trina. She never asked why I hadn't written her. All of her letters were sweet and kind, but it was the words in this particular letter that brought life back into my dying soul.

Dear Ken,

I hope you are okay. I have been thinking a lot about you, as I do every day. I don't think people really understand what war does to a soldier. With danger all around, I know you are afraid. I admire your strength and courage. I know it's not easy being far away from home. And I know you miss your friends and family. I watch the news a lot. You probably have seen more than you care to talk about, and you may never talk about it. I am proud to write you and tell my friends I know a brave soldier who's fighting in Vietnam. Just remember, I'm here if you need me. I will listen. You have a friend.

Warmest affection, Trina

P.S. I have enclosed a portrait of me.

She wrote as if she was right beside me. She came into a soldier's world—my world. Her letter bore no news of herself or what was happening back home. In this letter, she thought only about me. She seemed to understand what war could do to a soldier. For that, I was grateful.

A small photo of her was between the folded sheets of paper. I studied the stunning portrait. Her big smile seemed natural. She'd tilted her head slightly to the side. She looked calm and peaceful. I wondered what it was like in her seemingly quiet, undisturbed world. I flipped on the back and saw where she'd written her phone number.

I had no intentions of becoming seriously involved with another woman even though I found her letters comforting. I had my guard up. No one was going to get to me like Ava had. I was fighting to never fall in love again. And I was sure I'd win.

CHAPTER 16

It was time to return to our fortified positions. About dust, we went about two clicks from our compound to set up an ambush. If the enemy moved toward us, the flares we set would notify us that they were in our KZ. Two of our men went on guard duty while the rest of us slept.

Each time I dozed, Nate would start talking. He wanted to talk about his new girlfriend from the village. I kept silencing him. He didn't have a clue about the danger in the bush. We veteran soldiers knew that anytime an ambush was set up, not to talk much. Even our whispers may be too loud. And when it was very quiet, above the jungle's natural sounds, the slightest movement in a bush could be heard. We also cautioned the new men to hold their nicotine cravings. The greatest mistake any soldier could make was to strike a match. The small spark could be seen from a very long distance and easily give away our locations.

The mosquitoes were terrible that night. I sprayed so much bug spray that I caught a headache. I sat in the thick vegetation of trees and daydreamed about Trina. I wondered how it would feel nestled with a woman on her sofa or at the lake in my old Ford jalopy. Her magical smile on her portrait was priceless. It was as if she was saying to me, "It's okay to love, again".

We stayed low in the cluster of shrubs, watching carefully for poisonous snakes and other dangerous creatures.

The night wore on with sounds of the jungle that gave me the jitters. I never knew if the sounds were from jungle wildlife or from a signal from the enemy. We stayed low in our positions until daybreak.

Early that morning, our luck ran out. I heard movement around us. Seconds later, incoming mortars hit near our position. The rounds were coming quickly and shrapnel were flying in every direction. I heard one of our men yelp in pain, followed by silence. I was certain we'd lost him. The attack was short-lived with no more following it.

The next morning, we checked on everyone. Two of our men were wounded, but none of us were killed. I worked my way to the wounded and helped carry our men out of the field. It was hard to look at their twisted faces as they tried hard to bear the pain. Recalling that terrible day when I got wounded in the Triangle, I clearly understood what they were going through.

Later on in the week, we continued working from the bridge. It wasn't far from our fixed position. The 11th Armored Calvary was somewhere nearby. They were our support unit and ready to come to our rescue when we needed them.

Nate kept telling me that he wanted to go back into the village and find his girlfriend. I cautioned him, again, but I knew he didn't hear a word I was saying.

A few minutes later, I missed him. He'd slipped away quietly. I turned to one of the soldiers.

"He knows nothing about this life," I said.

The soldier laughed.

"He's gonna be fine," he said. "It's like shopping for shoes. You walk in a store, see what you want, find your size, and bam! You're finished."

Several of the guys laughed with him. I knew then no one felt like I did about Nate. He was vulnerable and probably thought he was in love. I knew better.

I found out that Nate had gone exactly where I thought he'd gone. The men at chow said he'd slipped off to see this girl. Each time he went into the village, he gave her anything she wanted. This time, they said, he'd not only given all of his money in his wallet, but he'd taken off his chain around his neck—the one he said his mother had given him on his eighteenth birthday. I shook my head when they told me. It was hopeless to get across to him.

One day, while I was standing outside of the village club with a couple of men, I saw her.

"There's Nate's girl," one soldier said as he thrust an elbow to my side.

I looked up. She was pretty as I'd suspected. But when I looked down at her feet, to my surprise, they were turned completely backwards. She walked with a limp. Her deformities, however, didn't seem to bother Nate at all. His face told the story. I had never seen such excitement and warmth in his eyes as I did that day when he looked at her. I knew when our time was up in Ben Cat, it was not going to be easy to get him out of there.

Jonas noticed the woman's feet and nudged me.

"Get a load of that," he said.

I didn't want her to catch me staring down at her feet, so I pretended to be preoccupied with a passerby. The men kept on whispering and glancing at the girl. She must have caught them making fun of her, because she acted as if she was in a hurry to leave. She tugged on Nate's arm. He threw up a peace sign in the air and headed out.

The bartender slipped me a bottle of whiskey. I popped the cap and filled my shot glass as I looked across at Jonas. His eyes were fastened to the door where Nate and his girl had disappeared.

"He's gonna have a hard time with that," Jonas said, looking bewildered. I knew he was referring to the mechanics of Nate's intimate evening with a woman of deformed feet.

"Somebody threw him a curve ball," he said. "How's he going to handle that?"

"I'm sure his encouragers will help him figure it out," I said.

"What?" he asked.

"Some guys have been pushing him on ever since he got here," I said. "They know he's a boot when it comes to women."

We didn't see Nate for the rest of the evening until we got ready to leave. He appeared and came out into the thick tobacco smoke room, tucking his shirt in his pants. A couple of men clapped. Nate looked around surprised. Quickly, I jumped to Nate's defense.

"Lay off him," I said, to the men.

"What's so funny?" Nate asked, glancing at their faces. The laughter grew louder. A soldier with a thick goatee put his deck of cards to the side. He hunched a guy beside him.

"Look at that face," he said.

"Did he strike gold or what?" The other guy said with a hearty laugh. A toothpick hung loosely in the corner of this mouth as he sat grinning.

"If you're talking about my girl," Nate said. "It's none of your business."

There was more laughter from the men. The toothpick guy leaned into his friend's ear.

"Can you picture that?" he asked. "How did you get those feet to cooperate? She's weird, man."

That struck a nerve in Nate. His face and ears turned beet red.

"She's not weird!"

I stepped up and took Nate by the arm, ushering him out of the place. He resisted and jerked away. His eyes glared at the men.

"I love her . . . and she loves me," he said. "That's all that matters."

That's it. He'd done it. He'd fallen hard just like I'd predicted. Nothing mattered but her. He seemed so innocent and so much in love—much like the way I was with Ava. But unlike what I had for Ava, I knew he was no more than infatuated with a real big dose of it. And there was no way I could get that across to him.

"She's got a man," the toothpick guy said. "You didn't know that?"

Nate looked hurt and shocked.

"Come on," I said, tugging on his arm. This time, I was pushing him to the door.

"I told you not to listen to these men," I said.

We walked out into the fresh air with the laughter and jesting of the men bursting behind us. Agitated, I took Nate by the shoulders and made him look at me.

"Didn't my talk with you about the village women do any good?" I asked. "It's a mystery to love. It doesn't warn you about the twists and turns in the road. It just lets you feel . . . feel its warmth, and embrace it. But you have to be careful. Two people need to have the same intensity of love and giving. If that's not happening to you, then her glass is full of your love and your glass might have only an ounce of hers."

He stared in my face. By the look on his face, he was confused or just not willing to hear me.

"Look, I don't want you to be like me," I pleaded. "I let someone have my heart for a long, long time. But, she gave her heart to someone else. You don't want to go through the hurt I went through."

I paused, hoping this time I'd gotten over to him. If he's listening, I thought, I would have done my job. If I could spare him from the depths of despair and the pain from a broken heart, then I figured I would have fulfilled my duty as a brother's keeper.

A few days later, Nate stayed longer and longer each time he went to the village. The girl was getting to him, and things seemed to be getting much more serious. When he returned to base from the village, I approached him

"So what did she tell you?" I asked.

"What do you mean?" Nate asked.

"Did she tell you that she loved you and she wanted to be your girl?"

Nate nodded.

"Don't you ever listen?" I shouted. He looked at me as if I had shot him in the chest.

"I'm in love," he replied without blinking an eye. "And I'm not going back home without her."

"You're talking like an idiot," I said.

His face flushed.

I scolded him hard for about an hour. When I saw I wasn't getting through, I gave up. That was the last day I brought up the subject.

My Rest and Recreation (R&R) was coming up soon and I couldn't wait. I had about two weeks before I would take my leave for rest. I cherished the day I'd go to Hawaii.

After several days, and I got up enough nerve to write my first letter to Trina. The words were clumsy at first. I kept balling paper and tossing it. I didn't want to say anything that sounded foolish. Writing a letter to a woman I met through mail was not easy. Finally, I wrote from my heart.

Dear Trina,

I'm sorry it's taken so long for me to write. We've been in the field for about weeks, now. I just got back on base. However, I've been thinking of

you a lot. Please don't stop writing. You will never know how wonderful it feels to read your words on those sheets of notebook paper. I will always treasure them. I think of you every day. Until I meet you face to face, take care of yourself.

Ken

I placed the letter inside my shirt and prayed I wouldn't chicken out and not mail it. When morning came, I hurried and dropped it into the outgoing stack of mail.

The week before my vacation, I went to the club. For the first time, I decided to watch a movie. We didn't have a lot of American movies. However, the ones we had served the purpose of good entertainment. I tried fighting sleep, but after ten minutes into the film, I had dozed about a dozen times. I was more than ready to go on a much needed vacation.

I knew the first thing I wanted to do when I landed in Hawaii was to get an American-made hamburger. The second thing I wanted to do was to call my parents and then Trina.

I packed my bags that night, thinking about leaving my men. I felt sorry for the fellows I was leaving behind for my R&R. The weeks in the field were torture. All of us deserved a break. Their time would come like mine, but without me, there was one less man to fight. I fell asleep thinking about their next mission. I had troubling thoughts of the many that would die while I was away.

Finally, daybreak came. I gave my duffel bag a final check to make sure I'd packed all the necessary items—cigarettes, shaving kit, boxers and T-shirts, ChapStick, lotion, and my canteen which held my whisky. I also found a few crossword puzzle books my mother had mailed to me..

I saw Jonas standing outside. I hurried over to him.

"It's a great day!" I said.

Jonas laughed. "Don't try anything crazy in Hawaii,' he said.

It was tempting. There had been reports of men not returning to the war after leaving for their R&R.

I gave Jonas a quick shoulder hug and hurried to the chopper.

The day was hot as usual. I was sweating big drops of water by the time I boarded the chopper. It didn't take long to fly into Saigon. And from there, I climbed aboard an aircraft for Hawaii. Having spent countless weeks on a chopper, the sight of an American passenger plane was beyond words. I found a window seat and settled down.

As soon as I got comfortable. It felt like ten tons of weight had been lifted off my body. Staring out of the window, I watched as the ground drew farther away and the jungle looked like a patch of greens in a veggie garden.

Succumbing to tiredness, I closed my eyes and tried to block all of the images of the war and the horrendous things I'd experienced. The vacation would be short, and I needed every minute to feel like I was a civilian, not a combat soldier.

I thought a lot about Nate. He was left alone with the unpredictable events of the war and women. There was no one like me to watch him. Even though I tried hard not to let this white boy with red hair and freckles get next to me, he felt just as close as Connelly and Billy.

One day Nate said, "I've never had anyone to treat me like you do. It's like having a big brother who follows you to school every day so the bullies would leave you alone."

I wasn't trying to be a big brother, just his friend—someone who'd tell him the truth no matter the cost.

Hours later, I was flying over the city of Honolulu. As we descended beneath the white clouds, I peered out of the window onto the island. The view from the sky was breathtaking, more spectacular than I'd ever imagined.

The plane touched down to a smooth landing. I grabbed my belongings as fast as I could. A few passengers ahead of me blocked my path as they were greeted by their loved ones. Squeezing by them, I made my way through the terminal.

At last, I stepped outside into the bright sunshine. No typhoon winds, no blazing hot sun, and no incoming mortars to dodge. It was paradise.

I looked at the American tourists and natives. It took a moment for it to sink in that I'd left the ravage country of South Vietnam. Soon, I would grace the beaches, enjoying the aqua-blue waters like the ones I had seen in magazines.

I plowed my way through the crowd of civilians and tourists. I was edgy, jumping every time someone got close to me. The sounds of passing cars made me want to dive for cover. Instinctively, I kept looking around, anticipating danger.

I saw a sign hanging over the airport terminal that read "ALOHA." Everything soon felt unbelievably wonderful. I stood for a moment to take it all in. The soft winds brought the sweet fragrance of the city—not the smells of a ravaged country with the stench of raw sewage.

A taxi cab pulled up to the curb. I hopped in and gave him my hotel in Waikiki. Before long, he pulled into a tall, exquisite building.

Inside the lobby was a visitor's welcoming table loaded with assorted cookies, fresh fruit, lime/lemonade water, and coffee and tea. I grabbed a couple of chocolate chip cookies and headed to check in.

The desk clerks were exceptionally nice. A beautiful Hawaiian girl gave me my key and politely walked me to the elevators.

I stepped off on the seventh floor, stuck the key in my door and walked inside a nicely furnished, well-decorated and quite spacious room. Coming from the hooch, it looked exceptionally large.

First things first. I threw my duffel bag on the bed and headed for the bathroom. Having been in the boonies for weeks at a time, I couldn't wait to sit on a real toilet and, finally, grab soft toilet tissue instead of leaves from bushes and vines. I sat there looking at the fresh white towels and face cloths folded on the granite sink counter. I'd arrived to familiar surroundings, and it felt mighty good.

I tore off my clothes and stepped into the shower. The glorious warm water splashed forcibly across my back and shoulders, relieving tired muscles and stiff joints. Although I'd been grateful for the few showers I'd gotten from our hand-made, Tarzan-like stalls at base, there was no comparison to the real thing. While in the jungle, we had to pour water into our helmets and wet our faces to get relief from the heat. Except for the monsoon rains that kept us soaked, a hatful of water was about all that touched our hot, dirty bodies while on the battlefield.

About twenty minutes later, I had to force myself out of the shower, knowing that after my R&R, it would be a very long time before I would have the American way of living.

Standing nude before the mirror for the first time in months, I was able see my entire body all the way to the floor. I'd lost a few more pounds since basic training, and my crusty skin was darkened in spots from being exposed to the sun and heat. I looked closely at my face and noticed deep bags under my eyelids—a direct indication of sleep deprivation. I examined my side and arm where shrapnel had claimed. My wounds had healed, but there was a deep scar. And I still had difficulty raising my left arm.

I wrapped a towel around me and dropped into a chair. In seconds, I'd drifted off to sleep. I kept waking up about every half an hour and looking around. No matter how exhausted I was, my body had become accustomed to lack of sleep.

Around six o'clock that evening, I dressed and went out looking for some excitement. After I walked a few blocks, I flagged a cab.

"Take me to the best place of the good old nightlife," I said to the driver.

He nodded and drove me about five blocks from my hotel. We stopped in front of a building. It looked much like a small café. I handed the driver a couple of dollars and stepped out onto the sidewalk. A young couple with their arms locked brushed past me. I followed them inside.

The place was packed with loud, energetic party folks, mostly tourists it seemed. It was a malty-smelling room with a lot of men and women making their way back and forth to the bar. Upbeat American music blasted on the jukebox. I pressed past a few women on the dance floor with drinks in their hands. A moment later, I sat at the counter and ordered a beer.

My eyes were constantly on the entrance. As people walked in, I observed them closely, as if they might be disguised Viet Cong. Suddenly I felt uneasy. Even though I was far from the battlefield, I never stopped doing what came natural in combat—watching for trouble even though all of my surroundings suggested otherwise. I kept reminding myself I was in Hawaii, a peaceful place with smells of hibiscus and sweet plumeria blossoms— not Vietnam jungles with the smell of death.

The bartender put a glass before me and poured my drink. I took a big swallow and then another. It took only a few minutes, and I started feeling a buzz.

Resting against the back of my bar stool, I basked in the atmosphere while the soothing liquid traveled slowly down my throat. Even the liquor on the tropical island seemed to taste better than what was at base camp.

My eyes traveled the bar and grill. Costly tapestry hung on the walls. Asian and Western art sat on the shelves behind the bar. The music grew louder. Several couples joined the women on the dance floor. I soaked it all in—the people, the music, and the wonderful atmosphere of the club.

After a couple of hours, I decided it was time to call a cab. It was getting late, and I hadn't called home. I asked the bartender to call a cab for me.

Within five minutes, the cab was outside waiting. I had a taste for a hamburger, so I asked the driver where I could get one.

"Tula's," he said, as he started the engine. "About five or six blocks. You want to go?

I nodded.

He pulled off. The night was fantastic. I rolled down my window and looked into the heavens. There was not a cloud in the sky. I'd heard that the temperatures never fell below sixty-five or seventy degrees, a big difference from the extremely hot temps in the jungle. The driver stopped in front of a restaurant.

"You'll find the best ever in there," he said as he pointed to a building across the street.

"Wait for me," I said, as I hopped out and hurried across the street.

Before I walked in, I could smell the fried foods coming from the entrance. My mouth started to water. I was eager to get my teeth into that juicy, dripping with grease and mayo, stove-fried hamburger.

Shortly, after I found a booth, a middle-aged waitress with a black apron tied around her waist came over. I ordered the largest burger one on the menu.

"Will that be all for you?" she asked, smiling.

"And a beer," I said.

She turned and politely took my menu off the table. I sat and took in all of the sounds and mingled voices around me. The war had sharpened my hearing. I could hear distinct statements from a couple of females who sat two tables from me.

"We'll have to come back next year and stay two weeks," one lady said.

"With lots of shopping cash," another one answered.

They had the right idea, I thought. When you get in a place like Hawaii, you want to have time and money.

About ten minutes later, the waitress returned with my order, a triple-decker burger and French fries. Before she could hardly put the plate on the table, I reached for the sandwich and took a huge bite. Instantly, a sharp pain ran through my stomach. I grabbed my midsection and bent over. I couldn't speak. I pushed the plate aside and tried to stand, but the pain was too harsh.

The young girl looked concerned and offered her hand for assistance. I held my mouth and pushed her hand away.

"Do you want me to get someone to help you get to the restroom?" she asked.

"I'm okay," I said.

I tried to stand without bending, but to no avail. The waitress pointed to the direction of the restroom. No sooner had I gotten to the toilet, I threw up. I stayed there for about a minute before I could stand upright.

When I got back to my table, the same waitress was standing with a glass of water.

"Oh, dear," she said. "Are you sure you're okay?"

She handed the glass to me.

"I haven't had American food in a long time," I said, I took a sip of water and sat back down. "I've just come off rations and my stomach has to adjust, I guess."

She stared at me.

"I'm so sorry," she said. "We try not to make people sick."

"No apologies. It's not your food that's causing this," I said. "I'm feeling better now."

She nodded like she understood and walked away. I tossed my napkin over my burger and left frustrated that I couldn't enjoy what I'd waited so long to get.

When I returned to my hotel, I headed straight to my room for some peace and quiet. But it was impossible to sit still. Even the silence was foreign to me and took some getting used to. I kept expecting to hear mortar rounds.

After about twenty minutes of tossing on my bed, I decided to call my parents. My mother picked up on the first ring.

"Hello," she said. The sound of my mother's voice was wonderful.

"It's me, mama," I said.

"Oh, my goodness!" she said. "I can't believe it. Where are you?"

"Hawaii," I said.

She started talking fast. Before I'd finish answering one question she was on to another one. Then finally she called to my father.

"Kenneth, come here!" I heard her say. "You won't believe who's on the phone."

I heard her say my name and my father mumbled something as he made his way to the phone.

"Hello, son," he said, in his low voice. I could tell he was smiling by the sound of his voice.

"Hey, Daddy," I said. "How are you?"

"Son, are you all right?" he asked.

"I'm fine," I said. "I'm on my R&R."

"They came to tell us you had been wounded, but we had heard you got killed." He stopped short. I heard my mother in the background talking.

"What did you say Mary Rose?" he called to my mother.

He came back on the phone.

"Your mother wants to speak back to you," he said. "It's good to hear from you."

A few seconds later, my mother came back on the phone.

"I told your daddy when we saw those officers in the driveway that you were not dead," she said. "He was all nerves, but I knew what God had told me. You remember, don't you?"

"Yes, ma'am," I said.

"That you would be wounded, but you won't die," she reminded me. So far, her predictions were true, and I was thankful. But I was still in South Vietnam, and the aggression was not getting any better. I'd hoped her prophecies wouldn't fail me.

"I told your daddy not to worry," she said. "When God tells me something, I know it's true. You just remember that. God's going to take care of you."

After she gave me the scoop on church affairs, cousins, and what was going on in town, I reluctantly mentioned Trina.

"I met a nice woman," I said.

There was a long pause on the phone. My mother must have thought I was talking about one of the Vietnamese women. Quickly, I figured I'd better set the record straight before she fainted.

"It's a girl I met through the mail from home," I said.

"Oh, well . . . then," she said. "How did you get to know her?"

"A friend introduced us by mail," I said. "I want you to call her and introduce yourself. I think she'd like that."

"Is she someone I'd like to know?" she asked.

"Knowing you, I believe so," I said. I fished in my duffel bag for Trina's phone number and read the digits to her from the back of the photo.

"Call her," I said. "And then tell me what you think."

"I will," she said. "Son, it's so good to hear from you. Be careful, you hear?"

We hung up. I longed for home more than ever. I reclined on my bed and pondered whether or not to call Trina. What would I say? What if I made a fool of myself on the phone by saying something dumb or boring? I was afraid to speak with her, to hear her voice. As much as I wanted to start over, I wondered if it was the right thing to do. What if I put my heart out there and it got crushed, again?

I didn't go to church much, except for holidays. As I sat there in the quietness of my hotel room, I thought about the one day I decided to go. I had sat in the back of the church. My mother stood in the pulpit with her bible. At that time, in most traditional churches, women were not permitted to speak in the pulpit. But my mother had joined this Pentecostal church that had welcomed her. She could speak as freely and as frequently as she wished. To the best of my memory, she walked from behind the podium that day and leaned into the audience to make her point. "It's better to face your demons," she said. "Go to what you fear, and the devil will flee."

CHAPTER 17

Later on that night, after wrestling with whether or not to call Trina, I decided to do it. I figured if she probably had already finished supper. It was after eight o'clock on the east coast. I took a deep breath as I pulled out her number and dialed. The phone rang three times before I heard a soft voice.

"Hello."

My heart started thumping wildly. I paused a second before I responded.

"Is Trina home?" I asked, as I clutched the phone tightly.

"I'm Trina," she answered. Her voice sounded like I'd awakened her.

"This is Ken," I said.

Instantly, she perked up.

"Kenneth! How are you?" she asked. She responded with such enthusiasm that it took me by surprise. "Where are you?"

"In Hawaii. Is this a bad time?" I asked. "I can call back."

"Oh, no . . . not at all," she said. "I was watching TV and dozing."

At last I could put a voice to the picture. It matched her portrait—kind and sweet sounding and medicine to my ears.

"Are you on your way home?" she asked.

How I wished that was true! Seeing her would be all I needed.

"No, not yet," I said. "I'm in Hawaii."

"So, you're in the states," she said. "That's so good to know."

We talked briefly about Vietnam until I decided to change the subject.

"Thanks for your letters," I said. "You don't know how good it was to see them when I returned to base, especially after being in the jungle for weeks at a time."

"I enjoy writing to you," she said.

There was a long pause. Neither of us knew where to go from there.

"I can't wait to see you in person," I said. "Even though your picture is incredible, I'm sure it doesn't do you justice."

"I hope you won't be disappointed," she giggled.

"I haven't been so far," I said. "I have only about four months left before I get out. I'm looking forward to meeting you.

I believe that was what she was waiting to hear. Exuberantly, she told me about plans she'd started making for me when I got home.

"Everybody knows about you," she said. "I mean not everyone, precisely. Just my close friends and mother."

"I hope you haven't built me up too much in their eyes," I said.

"Everything I told them about you is true," she said. I could feel her smiling.

"And what's that?" I asked.

"You sound kind," she said. "But not interested in a relationship so they won't push you too hard." She laughed.

"Well, now I have nothing to worry about," I said. "You're making it real easy for me."

"You bet," she said.

She giggled a lot. And when she laughed, I imagined a huge smile lifting her ruby cheekbones, as in her photo.

We talked a few minutes. Then we ran out of things to say. If there ever was a time I wanted to forget everything and catch the first plane for home, it was then. I had to remind myself that I was a combat soldier and would be returning in only a few more days to continue my assignment.

When we hung up, it felt like a ton of sand bags had dropped off my chest. A warm sensation flooded my heart. I undressed and slipped under the covers. I rehearsed our conversation as I pulled her picture from my bag and observed her. Putting a voice to the picture made it even more real for me—that there was someone waiting in America to see me when I returned, someone that seemed sincere and anxious with no personal agenda.

Suddenly, torturing thoughts crept in my head. What if I got it all wrong? What if she's not the kind of girl I imagined? I was beginning to wonder if there was something down the road waiting to challenge me.

I stretched out on my bed. At last, I was resting comfortably. The sheets and pillowcases were fresh as the morning dew. I studied the details of the room. The draperies partially hid the evening sunset, permitting only a small ray of light through the window. I thought to turn on the TV, but I changed my mind. The solitude needed no disturbing. Morning would soon arrive.

The second day of my R&R, I rented a green colored Dodge and toured the city of Honolulu. Vibrant green foliage from the fertile soil covered the roadside and valleys. I took it all in— the lush rain forests to the volcanic deserts.

After about an hour and a half, I'd had enough of sightseeing. I parked and found a pathway to the beach. Drawing near, I could see the white beach with its glistening waters beckoning me. The warm turquoise water, the lovely palm trees with huge leaves swaying from tropical breezes like ballroom dancers, and the magnificent sun was perfect for lovers. For half a minute, I thought this would be a good place to live, except I wasn't a huge fan of the storms that came with the islands.

I stepped into the water and traveled enough distance for it to come above my ankles and to my knees. My feet were clearly visible. I stood for awhile, gazing into the water. The ocean was quiet—almost too quiet for comfort.

It wasn't long before I walked back to the shore and dropped onto the sand. I'm not sure how long I sat there captivated by the islands charm. But when I looked around, a considerable number of people had gathered their things and left for the day.

I stayed on. My imagination shot ahead to Trina. She had mentioned her fondness for the beach. My fear of a lot of water could be a problem if she was a beach fanatic, I thought.

A plane interrupted my thoughts as it landed at the nearby airport. I shuddered and instinctively felt a sudden jarring to run for cover. Surprisingly, the effects of the battlefield were prominent, even on the quiet beaches of Hawaii.

After I'd exhausted myself in the sun, I gathered my slippers and wind jacket and headed back to the hotel.

Later on that evening, I wanted to find some action. I asked the clerk at the front desk if she knew where I could go and have some fun.

"Oh, yes," she said. "This group, Sly and the Family Stones, will be performing tonight on the beach front."

They were one of my favorite R&B recording artists. I rushed back upstairs and took a shower. Around eight o'clock that night, I drove to the place. It was loud and jam-packed. The band had already started performing.

I found a table near the back against the wall and got comfortable. The lead singer looked like me after I'd had too many beers. He made a couple of dance steps—a couple too many for his condition—and stumbled. He laughed at himself. Whether he meant it or not, his drunken behavior was much more entertaining to us than his singing.

I ordered a beer for starts. In about five minutes after I'd arrived, more people piled into the small, smoke-filled room until it was standing room only.

After a couple of drinks, I was feeling pretty good. Everything was amusing. I watched a white couple trying to swing dance on the floor. Their awkward rhythm made me think of Connelly and Billy when they tried to dance with the village girls. I chuckled to myself. Big Daddy was right. Even though he had joked about Connelly being a white man who had no idea of how to move to the beat, the couple on the dance floor was proving his point. The thought about that night when Connelly was at his best made me smile. It was the same night he and Billy apologized for their prejudice attitudes toward me. When I thought about them, the gruesome images of their fragmented bodies in the Triangle entered my mind. I had to shake myself and force the thoughts away. I gulped down more beer.

An hour later, I was tipsy and feeling it. I looked up and saw a young female, too lovely for words, coming towards me. She pulled up a chair and sat beside me. Dangling bracelets graced her arm with earrings to match. Her lips were smeared with thick red lipstick. As her eyes met mine, she spoke in a low, sexy voice.

"Hello, my name is Julie," she said.

I leaned into her to hear over the music and caught a whim of her sweet-smelling perfume. She touched my arm.

"I'll be back in a moment," she said.

Julie slid out of her chair. I watched her disappear to the ladies' restroom. My mind raced ahead, anticipating her return. "The company of a pretty woman in one of the most magnificent places on the earth is not a bad way to start a vacation," I thought to myself.

Suddenly, I felt a tap on my shoulder. A waitress looked down at me. "Just a word of caution," she said.

"That's not a 'she' . . . she's a 'he'."

My mouth fell open.

"What?" I exclaimed.

"Just thought I'd let you know," the waitress said.

I barely let her finished her statement before I slid out of my seat and headed for the door. I staggered out of the club and down the sidewalk. Around the corner, I saw a taxi cab and flagged it. My head was spinning. I was so intoxicated that I don't recall giving the driver the address to my hotel.

The next morning, I woke up sick from a hangover. At first, the night before was a blur. The only thing I recalled was getting off the elevator onto my floor and seeing a half-naked woman giggling as she sped by me. A man staggered with a smile as if he had plenty of time to catch up with her. He followed her down the hall into a room, and the door shut hard behind them.

The next morning, bright sunlight peeped through the blinds. I pulled the covers over my head, trying to go back to sleep. Slowly, the events of the night before came to me. I remembered the girl. She was just too pretty to be anything other than a woman. When I thought about what the waitress said, I laughed. I was happy she'd warned me. I might have brought Julie back to my hotel room. I laughed out loud at that thought.

I was so stunned at what the waitress had said that I'd forgotten I'd rented the Dodge and left it at the club. The hangover had my head pounding. I tried to pull myself out of bed. A bottle of Jack Daniel's was on my dresser. I poured a glass and stretched back out on the bed.

Four hours later, I took a cab back into town and found my rental car parked where I'd left it. It was embarrassing to know that in my flight, I'd rushed right past it. I turned the car in that evening. From that day until it was time to leave, I walked everywhere or caught the tour bus.

Time flew by. I had spent an entire week in Hawaii, and I still didn't get to see Maui and other places I'd heard about. Much of my time, I was drunk. I drank to get started. I drank to wind down. My drinking had gotten out of hand, and I knew it. However, I couldn't seem to put the old friend away.

Five days out of Vietnam helped relieve a lot of anguish and stress. Nonetheless, I had to shift gears. I had to remind myself that I would soon be returning to the jungles.

It was a great week. I dreaded leaving Hawaii. Although I was still fatigued, the trip had given me enough wind to return and continue my duties. I caught a flight to Saigon and boarded a chopper that took me back to the base. When I got there, I was told my platoon was out on a mission.

The next morning, I joined them in the bush. When I arrived, the first person I saw was Jonas. We slapped palms and hugged. A cluster of other guys soon greeted me.

I looked back at Jonas and noticed a very strange look on his face. It wasn't one of fatigue. He looked troubled.

The men settled back down, but all of them seemed uneasy. I suspected they'd gotten orders to go back into the Iron Triangle and was reluctant to tell me. After a few seconds, I realized I didn't see Nate. Just as I was about to ask about him, Jonas sat down beside me. I looked into his eyes. A strange feeling crept over me and settled deep in my belly.

"What happened?" I asked.

His eyes were hallowed and sad.

"It's not good news." He paused in silence. I didn't have a clue what he was talking about. Since I'd been in the Nam, nothing was good news except when a mission had ended.

"Nate . . . he got zapped," Jonas said.

I was motionless. It felt as if someone had punched me in the chest with a hammer. There was dead silence among the other men. Each one waited, anticipating my reaction. It took a moment to get my breath. I turned to Jonas.

"What happened to him?"

"We were in the bush," he said. "The platoon halted for a break. Nate got some fool notion and walked too far away from the platoon. He stepped on a damn mine, man! The blast from the explosion blew him apart." He pointed to Garcia, a young Latino, standing across from him. "He's Nate's replacement."

I sat there, shaking my head. I felt like an alien in a foreign land or a character playing a part in the movie like *The Twilight Zone.*

"Are you okay?" Jonas asked.

I nodded. But I was not okay. Nothing made sense to me anymore. Why Nate? He was the most innocent, likeable guy of all I'd meet since I arrived. That news hit me harder than the death of Connelly and Billy. But I couldn't cry. That was the bad part. There was an ache inside that I couldn't explain or release, but tears were trapped inside of me with nowhere to go. Because I had left Nate, I felt an enormous sense of guilt. Whatever compelled him to walk that far out was beyond me. But, as much as I tried to think nothing like that would happen, I knew it was just a matter of time. He was bound to make a careless mistake.

A couple of minutes later, I mumbled. "Another good man is gone . . . just like that." I looked up into the faces of the men who were standing around me. They nodded.

Not a minute after my arrival, I had been jolted back to reality. I was back in the cruel, devilish pits of South Vietnam—hell on earth.

That night, flashbacks of Nate crossed my mind. I could see him standing in front of me with his blushed red cheeks and squinting eyes when I told him to stay away from the women. I thought about the innocent look in his eyes when the men teased him about his sex life and his stubborn jaw when I told him that the girl only wanted his money.

The next morning, I wrote Nate's parents to tell them what a fine son they had and how very fortunate I was to have known him. I recalled the good times and laughter all of us had with him.

Two days passed, and all I could do was think about Billy, Connelly, and Nate. I relived the emotional wounds. Damn this war!

CHAPTER 18

The following week, I got another package from my mother. The timing was perfect. I was down in the dumps that day, feeling somewhat nostalgic for home. Jonas watched as I plowed through the boxes of toothpaste, cookies, and toiletries. His eyes widened when he saw two bottles of hot sauce.

"That's what I'm talking 'bout!" he said, staring at the bottles.

He pulled each bottle out and kissed them. "Your mama's made my day."

"Mine, too," I said, jerking the bottles from his hand.

"C'mon, man," he said. "I'm hooked on this stuff. It'll taste so good on that buffalo meat."

As much as I despised doing so, I had to share my sauce with Jonas, another spicy food addict. I handed him a bottle. He sat back and folded his arms with a satisfied look on his face as if he'd just scored a touchdown.

"I'm sure gonna hate to see you leave," he said. "Just tell your mom she's got another son over here, so she'll keep on blessing me."

"Believe me," I said. "She's gonna know the difference."We both laughed.

The shorter my time got in Vietnam, the more I struggled to hold up under pressure. When I felt like giving up, I'd think about getting home to meet Trina. I thought about the things she'd mentioned in some of her letters—enjoying the beach, walking in the park, and listening to jazz. They were a few of my favorite things, too.

I did the usual that day—cleaned my equipment and headed straight to the NCO club. It was refreshing to have two to three days at base for rest even though there was always guard duty. One night out of the bush was like taking a vacation at a luxurious sea resort.

I walked into the club while a song was playing on the jukebox. The lyrics were "*Jimmy Mack, when are you coming back . . .?*" It was the right song for that moment. I marked my calendar after I returned from R&R. I had only twelve weeks left in Vietnam, and it couldn't come soon enough.

In one of Trina' letters, she mentioned she'd talked to my mother by phone and they were getting to know one another quite well. I smiled. I knew if my mother grew fond of her, Trina was already in the family.

I told Jonas about it. He laughed out loud. "If your mother likes her, you're at the goal post!" he said.

"All I can think about right now is staying alive so I can get out of here," I said.

From the day I arrived in Vietnam, the unexpected continued and freaky accidents just wouldn't stop. I recalled one incident of friendly attack. It was a hot, muggy day. We were sent out from out base camp Tru Duc on another mission. We were commanded to break off and go in two different directions. Somehow we got our directions mixed up. Even in full sunlight, the jungle was very thick and dim. Suddenly, some of our men heard activity from my group's direction. Assuming it was the enemy, they launched fire. We all started blasting anything moving around us. When the RTOs made the discovery, it was too late. We fought blindly for about three minutes before we discovered a grave mistake. We were firing on each other, again. It was a very intense fight, but luckily none of us were killed. Later on, we learned that someone had shot the wrong coordinates on his compass. As a result, this caused us to collide. After that incident, we took precaution to double check, making sure our course of direction was precise.

I began to wonder if the war would ever end.

It didn't seem to matter to the White House how we felt. Regardless of the opposition from anti-war protestors, we remained in the country. There were promises from the general in command that in time, the battle would bring victory. Despite the promises, the draft continued to pull hundreds of young men like me from their families, jobs, careers, and dreams.

The anxiety heightened in every class—the young, old, rich and poor. According to my mother's letters, my father watched the news and kept her up-to-date on the conditions. I knew he would keep a close watch on the war. Over 500,000 troops were stationed in the regions bordering South Vietnam. Men were dying daily by the hundreds. I was terribly fearful of becoming a statistic.

In the following days, good news came our way. We heard we would be pulling about two more weeks of guard duty at base camp in Quan Loi. Not having to go into the field was a blessed relief and long overdue.

Before the week was out, I got the best news I'd ever heard in my life. I got my papers for home. When my CO walked up with a smile, I felt like a kid at Christmas time getting his favorite toy he'd always dreamed about.

"Well, soldier," he said. "Here are your orders."

"I never thought I would see this day," I said, fighting tears.

I took the papers, but I felt a bit jittery afterwards. What if I didn't make it out? What if I stepped on a mine? What if I got killed from incoming mortar blasts? There was no fix course on what would happen on the battlefield or in the sky. What if some freak accident fell upon me like that of my lieutenant— the one whose head was tragically lopped off by one of our chopper's rotor blades.

I slumped down, clutching the papers to my chest. "Oh, dear God! Help me make it," I whispered to myself.

Jonas asked, "What do you plan to do when you get back home?"

That was an easy question. I just wanted to kiss the earth the soil on which I was born. I wanted to see my family once again. I wanted to see the new love in my life. Surprisingly, I also wanted to go to church.

As my time to leave got close, the days seemed to creep along. It seemed like it had been ten years since I first arrived in the ravage torn country, but it had only been ten months.

Weeks passed and guard duty seemed to be going fine. No major problems developed. But the calmness could change in a moment's notice, I thought. Our job was to keep alert, because the enemy was full of surprises. I was on pins and needles. I tried to hold myself together and shake the fear of losing my life, but it was impossible. I thought about it all the time.

On one particular day, we were eating in the mess hall and a siren went off. We took cover. The incoming rounds hit closer than we had anticipated. After the attack was over, I couldn't stop trembling inside for hours.

Conditions worsened in the jungle. The monsoon rains never let up, and neither did the fighting. We slept in knee-deep, wet trenches with only a poncho to shield us from the cold water. I discovered that if I kept still, my body heat would warm the water. This would allow me to bear wetness for awhile.

The mosquitoes were twice as large in the monsoon season. When they dived on our flesh, they'd suck blood like vampires. There were other insects just as bad as the mosquitoes—the bloodthirsty leeches. Once they attacked, they would cling tightly to the skin, making it impossible to ignore. We took turns plucking them off each other. Insect repellent was our best friend.

Rain continued for days at a time. My feet were constantly soaked. Due to the thick water blisters that kept forming, every step I made led to excruciating pain.

I would've lost my foot if it hadn't been for the medical doctor visiting our base. He came out to the field to examine us. When he saw me limping, he called me over. I didn't know how bad the condition of my feet was until he took one look at my feet and began to cuss.

"What in the hell is this!" he yelled.

He said my feet had some kind of jungle fungus. I watched him remove layers of dead, raw meat from my left foot. There were sore spots that pained me when he touched them, but that pain felt nothing like what I'd been walking and running in. It hurt to take the weather-beaten and cracked boots off, but it was twice as painful to put them back on.

The medic left me and went straight to my CO. I overheard him telling my platoon sergeant about my condition.

"How did this happen?" I heard him say. "That soldier is about to lose his foot. I'm ordering him out of the field until he's fully recovered. No soldier should be sent out on an assignment with his feet looking like that."

He walked off mumbling to another soldier. "I don't want to see that shit again!"

At last! Someone could see what a hellish situation we were fighting in and would do something about it. It didn't seem to matter to our CO how we were surviving out there. Instead of sending us new replacements, he was adamant on using the men already in the field, regardless of the consequences.

Not long after the conversation with the medic, my CO knew I was a barber and pulled me from the field to cut hair. I felt like a bird that had just been let go from its cage. It felt better than my R&R in Hawaii. I knew I was not out of danger, but my chances of getting my brains blown out had lessened somewhat. I had less than twenty days in the country before I'd go on leave, still mindful of the uncertainties.

The men were eager to sit in a chair on base to get a haircut, and I was eager to do it. I was out of the field—not in the hot, swampy rice patties, not swatting mosquitoes, not pulling leeches off my skin, and not hunting for the enemy.

By the end of November, the rain had subsided. The monsoon season had come to a halt. The hot blazing sun was upon us once more. We were from one extreme season to another. I'm not sure which one was the most torturing, the sweltering heat that kept my mouth dry and skin cracked, or the heavy rain water trapped in my boots that caused blistering feet and mud holes so deep that we found it tough to walk or run. Both felt like a living hell.

One evening, I walked outside. Jonas saw me and asked if I wanted to join him for drinks at the club.

"Don't feel up to drinking tonight," I said.

He looked shocked.

"Well, I'll be damned. Did I hear you right?" he asked.

I nodded. It was the first time I'd refused a beer or liquor in months. I didn't stop drinking altogether after that, but I certainly drank less leading up to my departure. I wanted to see that marvelous Freedom Bird bound for the sweet USA in a sober state, not a drunken one. The men started teasing me about leaving."He can't wait to see that woman," Jonas said, as he chuckled. "When we hear from him again, he'll be a married man with six or seven children."

"And so damn henpecked that he won't know his name!" someone yelled.

They laughed, but I didn't care. I was concerned about only one thing—seeing to it that I stayed clear of gunfire until I was whisked off in that glorious chopper headed to Saigon and then to the wonderful land of the United States of America.

The night before my departure, the guys and I celebrated at the club. I danced to the jukebox playing songs I remembered from the states. I pulled a girl on the floor. I was dancing and not staggering for a change. A tumult of laughter and congratulatory yells erupted from the men who were celebrating my leaving. One of the fellows poured beer and whiskey on my head until I was drenched.

I got back to my hooch and started gathering my personal items. My clothes smelled like a barrel of alcohol. I kept checking my duffel bag to make sure the discharge papers were still there, and I ran across a picture of Ava I'd forgotten about—the one in her bikini bathing suit. I stared at it for a little while, wondering if she'd married that guy.

I tore the picture I'd treasured for so long into tiny pieces and tossed them in the trash. I opened my Bible and the last letter I got from her fell out. For moment, I gazed at it, and then I reached for Trina's last letter that had revitalized my soul. On my cot, I spread the two letters side by side and observed them. I'd circled a line of Ava's letter, "I never want to see you again." Then, I looked at Trina's and read "I'm here if you need me.".

I lifted Ava's letter from the cot and balled it tightly in my fist and tossed it with the fragments of her picture. The pain was no longer there, tugging on my heart. I had finally done it. I'd let go of the haunting past with only one thought—to get on with my life. Through one woman I died, through another I was living, again.

I placed Trina's letter back inside my bag. I wasn't sure if I was ready to let down all of my guards and open my soul completely. But I knew I was not looking back.

I was up and ready well before the break of day. A few hours later, I was in the headquarters. I waited excitedly for the chopper. Everything I owned was tightly packed into my duffel bag—letters, pictures, and small souvenirs Cho Phi had given me were stuffed inside.

My mind rushed to my hometown. I imagined my mother standing at the door and my father rocking in his favorite chair. The old Rambler he always kept clean would be parked on the side of the house. I envisioned the neighbors coming out on their porches and shouting my name to welcome me back. Then I thought about Trina. How should I behave in front of her?

I said goodbye to the fellows. Each one of them wished me well. Jonas was missing, though. I asked about his whereabouts, but no one knew. I couldn't leave without saying goodbye to my friend, the one who changed my grave clothes into a tuxedo. "He has to show up," I thought to myself.

I walked out of my hooch and took a deep breath. It was hard to believe that I was finally going home.

My commanding officer appeared. "Good luck to you."

He shook my hand and rushed forward. Looking behind me, I saw the other men in my camp standing and waving their good-byes. It was a bittersweet departure. My eyes searched for Jonas, but to no avail. Then, out of the blue, I saw him breaking through the group of men.

"Hold up," he called. "You can't leave, yet."

I dropped my duffel bag and met him halfway. We clamped our arms around each other in a big hug.

Jonas was the hardest one to tell goodbye. He felt like my blood brother. My mind rushed back to the day I first met him. I didn't want any more buddy friends after losing Connelly and Billy. But after awhile, he won. I tried not to let him get inside my world, but there he was, like a night stalker standing at the door to my soul. I never thought this

Bridgeport soldier would become my rescuer in the war—one who held the keys to the door of my despair and would unlock it and break down the walls of my stony heart, but he did.

I might have revealed too much of myself, but it didn't matter anymore. I could laugh again.

I started walking to the chopper. Then I turned to Jonas one last time.

"You're waiting for your 'Thank you,' right?" I asked, laughing.

He grinned big.

"You damn right," he said.

"I'll send it to you in writing," I said. "That is, if you're right about her."

He gave me a quick wave as I boarded the chopper.

When the chopper lifted upward, unimaginable joy flooded through me. From the sky, everything below me looked different—like I was seeing the jungle for the first time. I noticed the blasted areas. The vibrant green hills were totally destroyed. I could see streaks of black gun powder and marks of mortar fire. I looked toward the camp that had been my home. Nothing at that moment was more painful than the memories of all of our fallen men. I blinked hard and looked away.

Soon after, the chopper landed in Saigon, and I went on to board Delta airlines for America. Only a few more hours, I thought. Then I'd be able to get a good hot meal, take a hot shower, and sleep in a real bed.

CHAPTER 19

As much as I tried to get a bit of sleep, I couldn't.

The flight was long and I was restless. I spent most of the night staring up at the ceiling or thumbing through a magazine. Finally, I drifted off.

It was around seven o'clock that December morning when the wheels of the jet hit the runway in Oakland, California. After twelve months of constant danger and fear, I was finally on the wonderful soil of my beloved country, the United States of America.

My mind went back to base camp in Quan Loi. I knew my unit was going out on another mission in ten days. Suddenly, out of nowhere, I felt anxious and sad. I couldn't really pinpoint the exact cause. During my flight, I didn't think at all about the men I'd left behind in the sunken valleys of South Vietnam. But there I was— sitting on a jet with no threats of war, feeling confused and disoriented.

The door on the plane opened. There were several other guys in the military that stepped into the aisle in front of me. I didn't recognize any of them. We looked at each other, nodded, and pulled out our duffel bags from overhead. Our nonverbal communication was all that was necessary. We clearly understood each other.

With my bag slung over my shoulder, I made my way through the terminal behind the other soldiers that stopped to use the restroom.

After taking the escalator, I finally arrived at the entrance and stepped outside onto the curb. There was a quiet breeze and a mild temp that day. I took in the clean, fresh air, feeling grateful it was a good flight. The busy sidewalk held travelers with Christmas packages and luggage. I didn't realize until I saw them that it was a few weeks before Christmas. I'd be home just in time for the holidays.

The other soldiers caught up with me. We engaged in small talk until a military bus appeared to transport us to the processing center. It was a normal military procedure called "processing out," a method similar to an exit interview when someone was leaving a job. We loaded our belongings, hopped in the vehicle and rode off.

The clinic was in Oakland—not far from the air terminal. A mental and physical exam was designed to measure cognitive and motor skills to determine if we were prepared to enter back into civilian life. If we passed, we'd continue on to our destination. I didn't know what they would discover about me. The thought of any type of examination made me uneasy. No soldier wants to be detained for further observations when he's that close to home.

There was talk about going into town after we'd finished our evaluations. I was all for it. I wanted to see everything that pertained to fun and excitement. But, most of all, I wanted some good American food. I heard they always fed us soldiers a T-bone steak meal as a welcome home gift.

We rode to a one-story brick building where our psychiatric evaluations would take place. It was the first time I could take a real look at the city—the condos, commercial buildings, the palm trees that gracefully lined the streets and citizens walking about seemingly without a care in the world.

When we got to the clinic, we walked into a room not far from the entrance. The small, tidy area reminded me of my visits to the dentist office when I was young. It held about eight chairs dispersed throughout, a couple of lamps, and scattered magazines on a table by the window. After being ambushed and pinned down under sniper attacks, I kept watching the door constantly. I figured it was going to take a long time for my paranoia to leave.

A middle-aged white gentleman wearing a plaid shirt and blue jeans had followed me inside. He sat down next to me.

A physician finally appeared. His eyes surveyed the men in the room. Then he disappeared into the back. We were there about fifteen minutes before he returned and called for the first soldier.

"I have a few papers to go over with you and some questions," he said to the soldier as he shuffled through a stack of folders. "Follow me."

An elderly man sat beside me. A newspaper and a crossword puzzle book were tucked under his arm. He introduced himself as Calvin Maylo.

"Just getting out?" he asked.

I nodded.

"Been to war?" he asked.

"Yes," I answered.

"Drafted or volunteer?"

"The draft got me," I said.

"I don't know anyone who has been drafted," he said. He looked saddened.

"But it's a shame how you, young people are dragged into a war you know nothing about," he went on to say. "Who got the notion to have a draft anyway? Some foolish Congressman, you think?"

I perked up. Someone was sitting next to me who clearly understood and felt the same as I did about the war.

"I hope to God this war does not go on too much longer without some kind of resolution," he said. "It's been going on too long."

He shifted in his seat as if he needed to get comfortable.

"They don't tell you everything in the news," he said. "How bad is it? Where is the heaviest fighting?

"It's bad everywhere," I said.

I knew that was not what he was looking to hear. He wanted numbers and places. But, that was all I wanted to say about the war. I didn't expect anyone to understand. I was exhausted from the mere thought of the battlefield. It would be a challenge to get back to normalcy, I knew that. I didn't want to revisit the hell I'd come from. Even the village with all of the stunning females and wonderful massage parlors was a place I wanted to forget. I didn't want to be reminded of the loss of my comrades, my friends and confidants. They were men who would never return to see their loved ones. Some had no family at all. Only the cruel grave would moan their deaths.

"Thomas . . . Thomas Kilpatrick," he said. "You know him?"

I shook my head.

"He's my neighbor's son," he said. "I think he was shipped over there awhile back. But he enlisted on his own."

"I was numb half the time and I really don't remember many of the men," I said. "I think I blocked it all out."

I lied. I remembered it all too well, especially the battle in the Iron Triangle. The fragmented bodies of Connelly and Billy crushed and lying in a river of blood, the look on my lieutenant's face before he drew his last breath, the awful cries from my men that I knew I couldn't get to in time, Big Daddy stumbling through the thickets with blood so thick that his face was unrecognizable, and Nate's stupid action that caused his death. The images were fresh in my head.

Mr. Maylo pointed to a room adjacent to where I was sitting.

"They take you back there and ask a lot of questions," he said. "But no matter how much information they get from you guys, they will never know the pain and misery you men are suffering in this damn, senseless war."

He kept on looking at the door to the room. Who's the one coming out of the war? I thought to myself. By the frown in his forehead and the angry tone of his voice, you would have thought he had been in South Vietnam with me.

"What's your rank?" he asked.

"Spec-4," I answered.

He stretched his hand for another handshake. I noticed his white knuckles that were aging. I could feel the warmth coming from him, and I appreciated it. There was nothing more comforting than having someone show you the utmost respect and kindness after returning from war.

The soldiers who flew out with me were sitting across the room. I glanced at my wristwatch. We had been sitting for about thirty-five minutes. Seconds later, I looked up and saw a man in a white lab coat coming out of the room where the examinations were taking place. I slid to the edge of my chair with hopes he'd call for me. He approached the front desk and said a few words to the receptionist. Then he headed back down the hall. Mr. Maylo kept on talking.

"Spec-4 . . . that's good," he said.

I nodded as settled back down. I stared in the pale face of the elderly man. He wore black-rimmed, owl-like glasses that hung on a chain around his neck. He struggled to get into the pockets of his pants. I watched as he pulled out a pack of cigars and offered me one.

"No, thanks," I said. "Cigars have never been my thing."

"Well, I guess I should never have stolen my uncle's tobacco when I was a teen," he said. "Of course, I don't think cigars are as bad as cigarettes. One of these can last me all day."

He pulled a newspaper to his face. I thought our conversation had ended when he crossed his legs. Moments later, he placed the paper down and turned back to me.

"Where are you heading?" he asked.

"Lenoir, North Carolina," I said. "I'm a mountaineer, you might say."

He nodded, and then pulled his paper back to his face. I sat quietly, hoping he was finished interrogating me. It wasn't my upbringing to be rude to the elderly people by ignoring them.

Another solder was called. He jumped up and hurried behind the receptionist.

"What's your full name?" Mr. Maylo asked.

"Kenneth Dula," I said. "Most people call me 'Ken'."

"Your parents living?" he asked.

"Yes, both."

"That's good," he said.

"My mother's maiden name is Patterson.

"Patterson?" he asked. "I know some Pattersons near Statesville, North Carolina.

"Well, you just might know some of my folks," I said.

He made me think of my mother's side of the family, and I smiled thinking about our family reunions. Each time we got together, it was more of the Dula family than the Patterson folks until finally it became the Dula's family reunion. I couldn't keep up with who married who or where they'd moved, and there were too many cousins to count.

Mr. Maylo pulled out a small snapshot of a petite woman. Her dark brown hair dropped to her shoulders.

She wore a pleasant smile.

"This is Linda, my wife," he said. "She has family in Statesville."He smiled, looking at the photo. Then he glanced up at the wall clock.

"I hope they won't keep you waiting too long," he said. "I know that you want to get on to your destination as soon as possible."

He couldn't have been more accurate with that statement. It was taking too long for them to get to me. There were five of us left to be seen.

"How do you feel about being drafted?" he asked.

I didn't know how to answer that question.

I reflected on Ava.

"I was numb," I said. "I guess there was so much going on in my life. There were times when I thought I'd lose my mind." I took my mind off Ava and went to Trina. "But thanks to the letters of a special lady, I got through it."

"Women have that affect on us, don't they?" he said.

Mr. Maylo studied my face. I sensed he wanted to hear more. So, I talked about the Vietnamese women, food, the massage parlors and anything else that didn't allow me to talk about the battlefield. Things like the weather, jungle creatures, and the monsoon rains. He got a good laugh out of hearing that some soldiers got a terrible itch from wiping their butts with the thick leaves of poisonous plants. He chuckled out loud as I described the buffalo charging soldiers and the joke about it always being a black man.

I looked down at the picture of Mr. Maylo's wife, which he still had in his hand.

"Your wife is very attractive," I said, hoping to change the subject.

"She's a keeper," he said. "We've been married forty-three years next month. I think the one thing that keeps our love fresh is that I married my best friend."

He turned and looked into my face with a serious look I'd not seen since we'd been talking.

"I don't know if you've ever been married," he said. "Or if you've ever been in love, but if you aren't married, and when you do look for that special woman, marry someone who makes you laugh. You see, life is like a dance of two people who enjoy each other. Because when the dance is just about over, she will remind you there's another one to come. And if the music stops—that is when trials of life take your smile, she will know how to turn your radio back on. So now, when the lights go out on the ballroom floor, I'll still be dancing to the music on the radio.

I sat in amazement at this man. He looked so ordinary, yet he spoke like he had lived on this planet before civilization.

Mr. Maylo took in a deep breath. "I do wish you well in your relationship whenever it takes place," he said, as he pulled out a crossword puzzle.

"Another word for lenitive?" he asked, as he stared at the page.

"Never heard of the word before," I said.

"If this is a way of proving my sanity or seeing if I'm capable of joining civilized people, I won't pass that test."

He laughed. "I'll be damned if I know, either."

I glanced at my watch. There were three more guys besides me who had not been seen. The day had been long. Suddenly, Mr. Maylo stood up and shook my hand.

"Thank you for your service, young man," he said. "You take care."

He made slow strides as he headed toward the exit. I don't know why he was there. I never thought to ask. But, there was something mysterious about him. It seemed odd he would be in a clinic for military veterans and that he would leave so suddenly.

"Specialist Dula."

I turned and looked into the face of a physician.

"Come with me," he said. I went silently into the room.

I underwent a physical exam and was scheduled for a psychological exam the next day. When I left the office that afternoon, the military bus was waiting. The other soldiers had already loaded up.

We headed straight to downtown. My stomach was ready for some fine eating. We found a restaurant in walking distance of where we were staying. I ordered a T-bone steak, loaded bake potato, mixed veggies, and a tossed salad with a buttered roll. To my surprise, my stomach welcomed the meat. It felt much different from my experience with my first hamburger in Hawaii.

We left there and went to a bar for drinks. It was getting late. Therefore, I cut it short and walked back to the barracks. Exhausted, I fell across my bed and went to sleep. It was midnight before I woke. I struggled to get undressed with every bone in my body aching. Finally,

I got down to my T-shirt and green boxers. Then I sank back onto the bed.

I woke around six that morning, awaking ever so often before daybreak. I crawled out of bed, stumbled into the shower and stayed under the water got cold. I jumped out with only a few minutes to dress.

The bus was on time and waiting to transport us back to the clinic for our psychological exam. Unfortunately, the exams only tested the obvious not the reality. I knew deprogramming my mental state would take some time. Perhaps, more time than I was willing to give it.

I was the first to go in. The doctor placed a puzzle in front of me to put together. Next, he asked a few questions about word associations. He then gave me a written multiple choice test. I left feeling pretty decent about the results. However, I knew not to get too comfortable. Anything could happen that would keep me from going home.

I hung around bars and cafés for a couple of days and then I went back for the results of my examinations. The doctor buried his head in his notes.

"Clearly, your hearing needs medical attention," he paused, as he kept flipping the sheets of paper. His pause was too long. I couldn't control my rapid heart palpations and clammy hands. My eyes were fixated on that folder in his hand.

From the blasts of artillery guns, I'd lost some of my hearing. But was it enough to keep me? What if he made me stay for more tests and observation which would delay my going home for only God knows when? I waited, dreading the doctor's final statement.

He placed the folder to the side and sat on the edge of his desk. "It's not enough to be terribly concerned about. And your psychological results are too troubling.

"What does that mean?" I asked.

He smiled. "I see no need to keep you from going home. You're discharged, soldier."

I grabbed hold of the chair to steady my hands. At last! The day had come. I stood up. The doctor reached for my hand and shook it. "Welcome home, soldier," he said.

I walked down the hall and greeted everyone.

My thoughts were immediately on Trina. I thought a couple of times about calling her, but I quickly changed my mind. I suppose I was stalling, being nervous about what I'd say. To be honest, I was just downright afraid. Nevertheless, the anticipation was mounting. Time was rapidly approaching, and we would have to see each other face to face. My insides did acrobats at the slightest thoughts of her.

The next day, I went off base to get breakfast. A waitress with her hair in a ponytail approached me.

"May I take your order," she said, quietly.

I wanted everything on the menu, but I settled for scrambled eggs, hash browns, sausage and pancakes. I asked for a side order of fried apples. I couldn't resist the apples as I thought about my grandmother's apples. Growing up, every time I'd go to her house, she would dice up green apples that fell right from the tree in her backyard. She would sauté them in butter and brown sugar and simmer them on her potbelly stove.

The waitress took my order and left. I looked around the restaurant. Not many people were there. But, after all, it was pretty early. My watch read, 6:23 am.

I thought about my family and wondered what it would be like seeing all of them. I imagined my mother standing in the doorway. Before I'd get my feet out of the car, she'd yell, "There's my boy!" She'd probably have all of her friends, none of mine, inside the house when I arrived.

A few minutes later, and my waitress interrupted my thoughts. My meal was in front of me. I stuck my fork in and ate like a hungry animal.

That evening, several of the men in the barracks wanted to go to the bar in San Francisco. I didn't need anyone to convince me. I was more than ready to paint the town.

The bar was crowded with lots of us GI's. Civilian women from around the city came in. Some arrived in small groups. Others came alone. They were loud and giggly— a rather pleasant sight for my eyes. A couple of the jovial females pulled soldiers from their seats, giving them an intentional come on. Although I'd just left some of the most beautiful women in world, the Vietnamese, I was delighted to see the face of an American woman.

I stayed out late with the men into the early morning hours. What a relief not to have a time schedule. No more one hour on and one hour off watch duty.

The next day, I was up before dawn and ready to leave California. Before I left the barracks, I called my mother to let her know what time I'd plan to arrive in Charlotte, North Carolina. She assured me someone would be waiting at the air terminal in plenty of time.

The flight was too long. I could almost taste my mother's fried rice and red eyed gravy. I imagined the fresh smell of country air and the sight of the wintry hills and mountains. I imagined seeing Trina and holding her in my arms. I held that image for a long time.

It was late evening when I arrived at Charlotte's terminal. I rushed to get off, anxious to see who would be my chauffeur.

I picked up my pace in almost a jog to reach the outside of the terminal.

My brother, Frank, and one of his friends were waiting at the curbside. They were grinning and laughing. I smiled back and rushed to hug them. My brother reached for my lightweight duffel bag and hurled it into the trunk of the car. By his orders, I sat in the front seat with him.

"Good to have you home, bro," he said, with a hearty laugh.

"You will never know how good it feels to me," I said.

He started the engine and sped off. Seconds later, he started catching me up on the happenings.

"While you were gone, the riots in the states were bad when we first heard of King's death," he said.

"Yea, you heard about our cousin being dragged to death by some white guys, right?" Frank asked.

I nodded. I didn't want to hear much about the violence from Dr. King's assassination. Leaving one war zone to face another was almost more than I could handle. And, I certainly didn't want to talk about it. I was sure everyone would tell me about it when I got home. However, Frank and his friend insisted on filling me in on everything.

The disturbances were not as bad, they said, but things weren't good, either. Blacks were still edgy and suspicious of whites. Frank started to go into detail about what happened the night my cousin was beaten, dragged and killed. The incident was too gruesome for me, so I politely changed the subject and inquired about other family members.

It was right about seven that evening when we arrived home. Frank pulled into the drive and parked. I stepped out of the car and heard a shout, like I anticipated, coming from her high shrill voice. "He's here!" My mother's outstretched arms met me halfway across the yard. On the porch, stood my father who gave his usual jolly chuckle, and then my sisters and brothers rushed out of the door. "Welcome home!" They said in unison.

I got plenty of hugs. Then my mother ushered me into the house. I stood looking at the happy faces as I inhaled the pungent smell of garden peas cooking on the stove.

"I know you are hungry," she said.

My father went to his easy chair in the corner of the living room while my mother talked for the both of them. All of my sisters and brothers were at home except for Leroy and Raymond. I was told they had gone to a softball game.

My other sibling never stopped talking. Each one talked over the other as if time would run out on what they had to say. Finally, when there was a break, my mother seized the moment.

"What is Vietnam like?" she asked.

"It's a fascinating country, especially Saigon," I said. "It's not a totally ravaged country like you hear on the news."

"Were you scared when you had to fight?" Rachel asked.

"Of course, he was," Thomas said. "Who wouldn't be?"

I looked into their faces. I never thought I'd ever see them, again. And there I was, staring in the faces of my brothers and sisters who used to get on my nerves, but now wishing they would get on my nerves.

I knew they wanted me to give details of my experience. They'd never know, I thought, how many times I came close to dying. And when I got Ava's final letter how I wished I'd died.

"Did you smoke any weed?" Rachel asked, laughing.

"If he did, he's not going to tell you, nosey," Shelly said. She turned to me and winked. I smiled. I figured that she, too, thought I might have tried to smoke a joint.

"Well, we're just glad you're home," Imogene said.

"Yea, 'cause I got tired of doing your work," Frank said.

"What work?" Rufus asked, with his eyes stretched wide. They all started laughing and talking over each other, again.

I slouched in an armchair and basked in the sound of their voices as I listened to all of the news about family, church, neighbors—you name it. I heard about church, our neighbor's near car accident, the baseball games, the unfair test grades, and the mailman who sent an IRS check to the wrong address. We laughed when Leroy said it was his name—one of his alias.

As tired as I was and as much as I wanted to be alone, their voices sounded like violin music of a professional symphony.

"There's gonna be a party for you," Imogene said. Her eyes sparkled like the morning dew.

"Now, I know you're tired, but everybody wants to see you," my mother blurted.

I nodded. I didn't feel up to the celebration, but there was no way I was going to deny my family the joy of celebrating my homecoming.

I got away, finally and stepped into the shower. I could still hear the laughter from my family while the water ran down my shoulders and chest. I pondered whether or not to call Trina with thoughts flooding my head. What would it be like to see her face to face? What would I say? Will I make a good first impression? She hadn't given up on writing me, so maybe she would be as eager to see me as I was to see her. I thought.

After about five minutes, I stepped out of the shower, dressed and went into the living room. My father had reclined in his favorite chair.

"How was your trip, son?" he asked.

"Not bad, Daddy," I answered.

He started telling me about people in town. He then went on to sports and the NFL playoffs. My father and I had many things we enjoyed, especially sports. As we talked, my mother would occasionally stick her head around the corner and add some unrelated subjects to our conversation.

I sat for awhile just looking at my father. His appearance was the same. He kept the regular style of his hair—a short cut, parted slightly on the left side. There were no signs at all of thinning. He didn't seem to have gained or lost an ounce. Everything about him was the same, even his short conversation. I don't know what I'd expected. After all, I'd only been gone a year even though it felt like a decade.

After supper, Frank and I went outside. Tubby ran from behind the house.

"Oh, my pal," I said. "You don't know how much I missed you." Tubby's tail was wagging a mile a minute. Frank tossed me a football.

"You still got game, man?" he asked.

"I can beat you at anything, now," I said. "Being home makes me feel like superman."

CHAPTER 20

I stayed outside a lot. Inside the house was too much activity. If too many of my sisters were around me at one time, I'd back away or leave the room entirely. One day, Imogene came to my room. She looked disturbed and concerned.

"You don't act the same," she said. "I know you had a real bad experience, but I didn't know you would be like this."

"Like what?" I asked.

"You don't want to talk much," she said. "And, you want to stay outside a lot. You act like we are a bother when we come around."

"Everybody feels like that?" I asked.

"All of your sisters and brothers," she said. "I don't know about mama and daddy."

"War changes you, sis," I said. "I don't expect anybody to understand.

"Well, we just want our brother back," she said, as she walked out.

I sat there getting agitated at myself for not being able to control the emotions I was feeling. I knew I wasn't the same. I wasn't sure if I'd ever be.

At my homecoming party, folks started arriving around seven that evening. I lingered in my room, wishing I didn't have to attend. I changed shirts a couple of times, read an article in a magazine on my dresser, and finally I joined them.

Familiar faces greeted me. They treated me like an Olympic runner who'd just won a gold medal. Friends of my mother and several people I didn't know at all hugged and kissed me. Afterwards, questions poured in. I knew it was going to be a very long evening.

My homecoming party was much like the one Ava gave me when I was leaving for basic training. I looked around the room. Except for Howard who had to work, my same friends were there. To my surprise, however, no one mentioned Ava's name. I suspect news had traveled, as bad news often can, that Ava and I had broken our relationship. I was relieved no one said a word about her. If asked, I had only one thing I'd say, and I could say it with confidence, now. "She's a thing of the past".

As folks poured in, good old-fashioned country food came with it. The table was spread with potato salad, yams, corn on a cob, turnip greens, fried chicken, ham and many more mouthwatering dishes from my mother's church friends. There was no room to put dessert in the kitchen, so my mother made her way to the dining room and cleaned off the buffet. She moved around the house with her head lifted like a proud peacock. I looked over at my father as his laughter filled the place.

Then out of the blue, in the midst of the merriment, I felt the way Imogene described me. I wanted to go to a room and sit by myself.

My mother kept filling my glass of her iced tea. She prided herself on making what she called the best in the world, and almost everybody asked for it when they came to visit.

Half way into the gala affair, she took me aside. Her eyes were filled with enthusiasm.

"Have you heard from Trina, yet?" she asked.

"I plan to call as soon as everybody leaves," I said.

My mother looked pleasantly satisfied and returned to talk with her friends. It dawned on me why no one asked about Ava. I suspected

Howard had told all of our friends, including those who were nosey enough to ask him about what happened.

The last guest left close to midnight. It was too late to call Trina. So, I talked to my brothers and sisters for about twenty minutes before they went to bed.

After helping my mother finish cleaning the kitchen, I went to the living room and fell out on the sofa. I must have fallen asleep as soon as my head hit the pillow, because I don't remember my mother placing a blanket over my feet, as she always did, and turning the light out.

A noise from the street woke me and sent me diving to the floor for my M60 that wasn't there. "You're not in Vietnam," I mumbled when I realized I was in my mother's living room.

I didn't feel safe feel anywhere. I kept waking up through the night from nightmares. In each dream, I was running in the jungle, fleeing from the enemy. They were all around me. It didn't matter which way I ran. They were there with rifles and guns. I would wake up from the nightmare and fall back to sleep, only to plunge into another bad dream.

A good night's sleep was foreign to me. During my time in Vietnam, I never could rest even when I had downtime. Every sound was disturbing. Even though sleeping on my mother's couch beat the rough cot and dugouts, it was hard to get comfortable. The ground had been my bed for so long that I couldn't rest on a bed or sofa.

After a while, I got up and went outside. I found a spot and slept with my dog. I felt safer out there with Tubby than inside. The outdoors permitted mobility. Inside a house or building was confining. I felt pinned in with nowhere to run.

When my mother realized I'd slept outside, she thought I needed psychiatric help. But my father knew what was happening to me. He told her to be patient and give me time to get adjusted. I slept outside with my dogs for three days. Before sunrise, I'd go back inside the house. My mother would always get up about fifteen minutes later and start breakfast. My sisters and brothers didn't know what to say to me, so they had little conversation. Frank never avoided me. He kept trying to find things for us to do.

Finally, it was the weekend when I'd see Trina. I sat in a chair in the living room early that morning and inhaled the familiar smell of breakfast. Before long, I heard my mother approaching my room.

"Bacon and eggs are ready," she said, nudging me.

The delicious scent of bacon and homemade biscuits was a long way from the buffalo meat and rationed beans.

At breakfast, I found out that a couple of my friends in high school had gotten married, and more strange cousins had shown up at our family reunion.

"I bet you didn't know you had a cousin over there in Vietnam," my mother said.

By what she described, he was in the "The Big Red One."

I was flabbergasted that a relative was there and I didn't know it.

After breakfast, to my surprise, my father offered his untouchable Rambler for me to drive into town. I jumped in it as fast as I could before he changed his mind.

Driving through Lenoir brought back a lot of fond memories. I spent a lot of time with my brothers going back and forth to town trying to find some type of excitement. The miniscule town looked quite different, now. In certain sections, renovations were made on some store fronts and new pavement on sidewalks. People threw up their hands as I rode by. I recognized some. Others were just the friendly old citizens of Lenoir.

I parked on the side of the street. Each time a loud vehicle passed, I ducked down in my seat. My CO warned me this would happen, but no matter how he tried to prepare me for shell shock, it didn't do much good. I understood why convicts, once released, would want to return to prison. As unpleasant as it was, I'd gotten used to Vietnam and knew what to expect. Home felt foreign.

I pulled back onto the street and drove off onto another. I approached Ava's place. I slowed down and pulled off onto the grassy shoulder.

Nothing had changed about the familiar brick apartment building. I stared at it and tried to imagine Ava standing in the doorway, but I couldn't bring a picture to my mind. I looked at the steps of the porch where we made our promises to never leave each other. I wondered if she was inside. Strangely, I had no desire to satisfy my curiosity. The past was behind me, and I had no regrets.

I put the car in drive and started to pull off when a car came up behind me. A familiar voice called.

"Hey, Ken!"

I got out of my car and saw my old friend, Eugene. He looked clean and well-groomed, unlike the shabby appearance he wore before I left. He stood tall with shoulders squared and a big smile.

"When did you get home?" he asked, shaking my hand and pulling me in for a hug.

"Last night," I said.

"Man, I heard about things over there," he said. "Pretty bad, eh?"

"That's putting it mildly," I replied.

"So, what is the president doing to get y'all back home?" he asked.

"Don't know," I said, shaking my head. "It looks like this war will go on for a long time."

"I was looking at the news and saw where nearly a hundred men were killed in one day," he said, shaking his head. "Now that's a shame."

The talk with Eugene brought back memories I wanted to forget. He talked about politics and the white house's reason for drafting. His voice held bitterness, the very emotion I was trying to rid myself. My heart had not grown hostile toward our officials. But in a lot of ways, I'd become angry and disillusioned about their lack of progress in getting us out of the country. Conditions worsened each passing day.

"And what I can't understand," Eugene went on to say. "Why do they keep sending troops over there knowing you're fighting a guerilla war, the worst kind of war there is? They need to bring y'all home, man."

He spoke similar words of Mr. Maylo as if he had heard our conversation.

"I just don't get it," he went on. He shook his head as he looked at me. His deeply lined dark face held despair as he waited for my response.

I felt hopeless. I had no explanation of any kind to give him. I could only think of the good that came out of the situation for me. Aside from the fact that I miraculously dodged bullets and mortar fire, there was an intangible, destructive war missile for which human eyes couldn't see that had almost destroyed my life—racial prejudice. My belligerent attitude toward whites had diminished. I thought about Connelly and Billy and the day we met. I recalled their stunned faces that held puzzling looks when they knew they'd been assigned to me who was obviously a black squad leader.

It still baffled me how close the three of us had become before the Iron Triangle. "You're alright, Carolina," Connelly said to me one day. "You feel like my brother. . . I mean, except for the color." I knew what he meant. He just had an awkward way with words. Our true brotherhood was undeniable. Then, along came another white boy, Nate, who was like a son to me. And, I thought of Big Daddy, my mentor and Jonas, the one man I had to thank for pulling me out of my world of frustration and lack of trust by turning me to Trina. Those things were the good I could recall of the war. Anything else, I'd rather forget. And, then I thought of Trina. I had Joe to thank for letting me see that living the life of a disillusion, broken-hearted, and grieving man wasn't getting me anywhere. I had to take the risk of opening my heart to receive love and acceptance from another female as scary as it was for me.

I followed Eugene to Kentwood Grill and grabbed a beer. We talked on the way about getting back into the things I used to do. I didn't know how I'd fit back into society, or more importantly, my community. The people had not changed that much, but I had. Eugene said most of my former classmates had moved away, and the hometown guys who were drafted with me had not returned from Vietnam.

"The factory jobs are plentiful, though," he said. I wasn't too concerned about finding work, because I knew if things got tight, I could always cut hair.

Town folks came in and out of grill. The ones who knew me congratulated me on my return from the war. I politely nodded and thanked them for their sincere regards. It was taking me longer than I'd expected to regain my poise for conversation. I didn't want people to continue probing me with questions. I don't think it ever registered with them that all I wanted to do was be left alone for a while. My CO's words echoed in my head, "It's going to be strange at first, and you are going to feel awkward trying to adjust back into society," he had said. "But don't get anxious. Time will take care of a lot of that."

Voices and laughter started to irritate me. That was another thing my CO had told me that was bound to happen. It was a part of being shell shocked, he said. I knew I needed the company of good folks with good conversation. But at the same time, it was nerve-racking.

I stepped out of the grill and headed to Howard's. It was about time for him to be home. I made my way across town and kept straight on route 321 until I reached his house. His Ford truck was parked in the driveway.

I hardly got out of my car when he appeared on the front porch. His face lit up when he saw me, and he started grinning.

"Man, you're home," he exclaimed, bouncing down the steps.

He rushed to me and gave me a big hug, lifting me off my feet.

"Come on in," he said.

I followed him inside. The TV was on in the living room. Howard hastily picked the remote up and turned the volume down. I sat down on the sofa. A throw was on the opposite end. His shoes and socks were kicked off, lying on the floor. A plate with scraps of food sat on an end table.

"It's good to see you!" He said.

"Same here," I said.

"Sorry, I couldn't make it to your party," he said. He pulled a straight chair from the corner and straddled it.

"No, don't apologize," I said. "It was a house full of senior citizens."

Howard laughed. He stopped and gave me an earnest look.

"I didn't write you, as you can see," he said.

"I know," I said. "She wrote and didn't waste time to get to the point."

"I figured as much," he said. "She told me she was going to write you."

I nodded.

"But guess what?" he said. "Jerome broke up with her. He left and went up north somewhere."

I was stunned.

"I thought they were pretty serious," I said.

"She might have been," he said. "But, Jerome had his own agenda, and it wasn't a long term relationship. He was all for a good time. That was it. As for Ava, she still lives alone. No one sees her much anymore."

"And, I have no need to see her, either," I said.

I met a woman I'm going to see in about two hours and twenty minutes.

"What?" Howard laughed out loud. "That's the best news I've heard yet!"

"After wandering aimlessly and wallowing in self-pity, I met this woman through mail," I said. I pulled Trina's picture out and showed it to Howard.

"What a beauty!" he said.

"We'll see how it goes," I said.

Howard had more questions for me than Mr. Maylo. I was smiling and laughing when I talked about Trina. We talked for about two hours before I headed back home. I rode with the radio blasting and my fingers keeping beat on the steering wheel.

The house was quiet when I got home. Everybody was gone except my father. It was still too early for Trina's train to arrive at the station, so I sat in the living room talking to him. He seemed very happy that I was home, and even more excited knowing he had me all by himself.

"You've made me real proud of you, son," he said. "More than you'll ever know. People don't understand the effects a war can have on you until they see that fitting back in to civilian life is not that easy. But you'll be all right."

It was a good thing that my father had been in the Korean War. I had someone who really understood how a combat soldier feels after returning home.

"You'll feel like you are still in the war, sometimes," he said. "And, you will be suspicious of everything and everybody. But, it'll get a little better after awhile."

My father was my hero that day. I don't think he realized how I needed to hear those words coming from him—a war veteran.

He got up to leave and turned.

"Good to have you home, son," he said, as he went to his room.

Several hours passed. Then the phone rang.

"He's been waiting to hear from you," I heard my mother say.

My heart started pounding. I rushed to the living room where she stood with the most gratified look on her face I'd ever seen.

"Trina is on the phone," she said.

I reached for the receiver. My mother walked away, taking hints from me.

"Hello," I said.

"Hi! How are you?" Trina answered, in a sweet pleasant voice.

"Good," I said. "Have you left yet?'

"Yes, we have a short layover," she said. "I'm about two hours away. I haven't eaten at all today. I guess I'm too excited."

"Don't worry," I said. "I'm taking care of that."

I was about to meet the woman who'd, undoubtedly, renewed my faith in women. By the sound of her voice, she was as anxious to see me as I was to see her. Her voice was enchanting and sexy.

I got off the phone and saw my mother standing in the kitchen waiting for me to come in.

"What did she say?" she asked.

"She said the train had stopped," I said. "It would be a few more hours before she would be in North Carolina."

My mother smiled, nodded and turned back to the sink.

Around 6:00 that evening, I showered, pressed my pants and shirt and put on some expensive cologne I'd purchased in Hawaii. I took a look in the mirror and decided I looked decent enough to make a good first impression. I put my watch on and headed out.

The two lane highway was heavily traveled from the evening rush hour. I turned the radio back on to help occupy my mind. I kept rehearsing what I'd say when we met, but nothing fit.

I drove westward into the sunset. A brilliant reddish-orange color with a hint of blue painted the clouds across the horizon. Watching the sky in its streaks of vibrant colors, I saw myself in its beauty. A once lonely, frightened and bewildered man was now saturated in streaks of peace, hope, and joy. The darkest hour is just before dawn, they say. I never thought I would come through the war, the darkest side of night, or ever see the breaking of day back home. A brand new day had dawned, and I was a brand new man.

A few more miles to go. My hands started to tremble. I could hardly hold the steering wheel. I slowed down the vehicle to stall for time. Finally, I made a couple of turns and I was there. I never thought a train station would look better to me than a tall, cold glass of Budweiser, but it did.

I found a parking space and got out, leaving the engine running. Leaning against my car door, I took in deep breaths. My heavy breathing must have been apparent, because I saw a lady looking at me. She smiled and looked away. I wiped my hands on the side of my pants and pulled out a stick of gum.

I heard the whistle. It started the jitters, again. I could see the front tip of the train in the distance. My heart raced as if it were keeping pace with the engine. I had wished to God I knew what to do to calm my nerves. I wondered if Trina was as nervous as I was.

Taking in a few deep breaths, I watched as the Amtrak finally approached the gate. The sound of the engine rescinded and the train halted. One by one, the passengers stepped off the train. I noticed several women with children and other passengers struggling with small pieces of luggage.

Then a couple of minutes later, I saw the lady that fit my photo. She stood for a second looking around. A scarf around her neck was blowing in the wind. She looked incredibly beautiful, more beautiful than her photo. I waved, and she saw me.

It was happening! A big smile appeared on her face. Then, as if someone had moved my feet without my permission, I rushed toward her. She moved with rapid steps in my direction. The scene was like something you'd see in a movie. Although we were only a few yards from each other, it seemed like we were moving in slow motion with miles between us. Finally, she reached my arms and dropped her overnight bag. I swept her off her feet in one big swinging motion. She giggled as I slowly lowered her to the pavement. We stood for a brief second, gazing at each other, both at a loss for words. Then a warm, sweet greeting fell from her lips.

"Hi," she said.

She offered her cheek for a kiss. My heart was still laboring.

I walked her to the car and opened her door. She slid in gracefully as I made my way to the driver's seat. We sat quietly. There was no script except what was written on the slate of my heart. Say it with silence, it said. Silence says it much better than words.

I didn't know if I was what she'd imagined or if I wasn't. Was I tall enough? Did my physique appeal to her? There was no indication on her face to tell me what she was thinking or what her heart was feeling. But it didn't matter. I felt liberated—no longer bound in the moment of time where life had lost its meaning for me.

I placed my arm on the back of the seat—perfect for her to snuggle.

"I want to hold you and never let go," I whispered.

She smiled.

WORDS OF KENNETH DULA

It was a long time before I was able to speak of South Vietnam and the letter from Ava that sent bullets through my heart and almost took my will to live. I was locked inside the prison of my mind. I thought I'd never love again, and it was unimaginable I'd live through the war. If I did live, I thought, I would never speak about Nam or Ava. But my best friend urged me to share my experience. I didn't think it would make much of a difference now since it had been so long ago. I was wrong. I discovered I became the voice of my fallen comrades—my heroes—who never got a chance to share their stories. The trenches held our secrets.

From time to time, I'd think about Ava. I was thankful I'd experienced falling in love with her, because of the lessons I learned of defeats and victories—that you need both to make you strong. Each one takes its separate path only to meet again to face yet another journey. I didn't think I would ever open my heart to love, again. But love found the path to my door and I let it in once more. I wasn't looking for love, but it was looking for me.

When I left the ravaged country of South Vietnam and arrived back home on the fertile soil of the United States of America, it was the best day of my life. I felt like a brand new man. I can't speak for all of the combat soldiers who were with me during my time in Vietnam, but I believe I can speak for most, both living and dead. If a soldier is blessed enough to return home, his first desire isn't to have an officer recognize him by the awarding of medals. It isn't the grand salute from the president of the United States who'd shake his hand in gratitude for the outstanding job he'd done, nor is it the look of proud family and friends. More often, it's the simple things he appreciates—a bed with fresh sheets and pillowcases; a good hot meal; clean drinking water; fresh air with clear skies—blue skies with no trace of black gun smoke hovering over. I appreciated all of that, but what I desired most was to see my new American woman. Her letters built a bridge over the troubled waters of my life. I was restored to faith and hope, but most of all, to feeling like a human being, again.

I tried to re-enlist and return to Vietnam, but having suffered injuries, I was prohibited from going back. Some people couldn't understand why I wanted to return to the battlefield. But war has a strange effect on a combat soldier. It was difficult to leave my fellow comrades in harm's way. We were more than dog tags. We had formed a great bond, closer than blood relatives, and we remained more loyal than a priest who'd taken a sacred oath to God. We went far past the color lines, making white, yellow and black skin one in the same. Connelly, Billy, and Nate were proofs. Amongst us were heart-to-heart conversations about our inner struggles—fears of dying, perplexities about the war, and trying to cope with heartbrokenness and loneliness.

A combat soldier knows this truth. He fully understands the contents on these pages and the indelible impact of love and war on a soldier's life.

As a Vietnam War veteran with a Specialty Title of Acting Sgt. E-5, Dula received the *Vietnam Service Medal w/one Bronze Service Star; Air Medal; Purple Heart; Bronze Star; The Army Commendation; Combat Infantry badge*; and the *Republic of Vietnam Gallantry Cross w/Palm Unit Citation badge.*

GLOSSARY

1. assistant gunner – a gunner (ammo barrier)
2. AIT – Advanced Infantry Training
3. article 15 – a form of punishment (no judicial)
4. AWOL – absent without leave
5. bird- refers to helicopters
6. body count – number of enemy killed or wounded
7. boonies – jungles or swamp
8. click – about a mile
9. brother – a black fellow marine
10. BS – slang for bullshit, or telling lies
11. bush – infantry term for field
12. C-4 – plastic, putty texture explosive use to heat C-rations in the field
13. Charlie – Viet Cong, the enemy
14. chop chop – slang for food
15. claymore – antipersonnel mine
16. cobra – an AH-IG attack helicopter (gunship) armed with rockets and machine guns
17. CP – command post for an officer in charge of a unit
18. C- rations – can meals for use in field
19. DEROS - date of estimated return overseas
20. dust off – evacuation by helicopter

21. firefight – a battle or exchange of small arms fire with the enemy (rifle fire)
22. Freedom Bird – a plane that took soldiers out of Vietnam
23. GI – government issued - an American soldier
24. gook – derogatory term for an Asian
25. gung ho – enthusiastic, usually about military matter and killing people
26. hooch – a hut or simple dwelling either for military or civilians
27. Iron Triangle – Viet Cong dominated area between the Thi Tinh and Saigon rivers
28. Jody – person who wins your lover or spouse away while you are in Vietnam
29. "John Wayne" – can opener
30. KZ – killing zone, area in an ambush where everyone is either killed or wounded
31. KP- kitchen duty, mess hall duty
32. LT – lieutenant
33. LZ – landing zone
34. M-16 – standard military rifle
35. medevac – medical evacuation out of the field to a hospital
36. MG – machine gun
37. nape – napalm, a substance used to waste the enemy
38. Nam – slang for Vietnam
39. NCO club – Non-Commission Officer's club
40. NPD – night perimeter defense
41. PFC – private first class
42. PZ – pickup zone
43. platoon – subdivision of a company consisting of two or more squads
44. R&R - rest and recreation, a three to seven-day vacation from the war

45. recon – reconnaissance going out to the jungle to observe or identify enemy activity
46. regiment – military unit consisting of a number of battalions
47. RTO – radio telephone operator
48. rucksack – backpack issued to infantry in Vietnam
49. short-timer – soldier nearing the end of his tour in Vietnam
50. shrapnel – pieces of metal sent flying by an explosive
51. squad – military unit less than ten men
52. strobe – handheld light for marking landing zones at night
53. TET offensive – major uprising from the enemy
54. trip flare – a ground flare triggered by a trip wire used to signal and illuminate the approach of the enemy at night
55. turtles – new replacements
56. waste – kill
57. weed – marijuana
58. LOH - military small helicopter (white bird)
59. WP – white phosphorous
60. zapped – killed

Made in the USA
San Bernardino, CA
17 November 2016